RAISED UP

Dead, Buried, and Raised Up!

Todd Tomasella

Raised Up

Copyright © 2012 Todd Tomasella

All rights reserved.

ISBN-13: 978-1475207361

SafeGuardYourSoul.com

Frisco, Texas

Visit www.SafeGuardYourSoul.com

© Todd Tomasella. All Rights Reserved.

Any part of this book may be reproduced, stored in a retrieval system, or transmitted by any means <u>without</u> the written permission of the author.

ISBN-13: 978-1475207361

Printed in the United States of America

All Scripture quotations deliberately taken from the Authorized Version of the Holy Bible, the King James Version

Cover Design by Bill Wegener: Colorenlargement.com

Do you desire to learn God's Word? – To begin receiving the *Moments with My Master* email that is sent out 2-3 times weekly, go to SafeGuardYourSoul.com and sign up. Or, email your request to: info@safeguardyoursoul.com.

Acknowledgments

May the LORD be thanked for all the friends He has given me who have helped by prayer and in a myriad of other ways. Those friends include ....

Aaron Moradi, Stephen Michels, Luanne Hisle, Bill Wegener, Travis Bryan III, Mark Case, Steve Turner, Kim Kininmonth, and many more.

Introduction

"For thou art great, and doest wondrous things: thou art God alone. Teach me thy way, O LORD; I will walk in thy truth: unite my heart to fear thy name. I will praise thee, O Lord my God, with all my heart: and I will glorify thy name for evermore. For great is thy mercy toward me: and thou hast delivered my soul from the lowest hell." Psalms 86:10-13

When we are quickened in the fear of the LORD, our lives will hasten unto the soon coming of the Son of God from Heaven. Those who fear God are hearing His voice as He is leading them in the lifestyle of the daily cross Jesus instructed us to take up. These remnant believers of Christ are living a life full of the Holy Spirit, being daily raised up in His divine power to produce fruit pleasing to Him and do His exploits (Daniel 11:32; Luke 9:23-24; John 2:24-25; 2 Corinthians 4:10-12).

Once you choose to obey the LORD and take up the daily cross, your feeble life will be exchanged for His. The joy of the LORD will fill your heart and life and the will resurrect you in His power; bringing you through every trial, temptation, and obstacle to His eternal glory. Let the addiction begin!

On Style......

Feeding Jesus' beloved sheep often requires instilling His truth into their hearts. In accordance with this guiding principle, there will be no hesitation to restate Bible verses in order to teach by repetition and association. This is because there are different occasions where the same verse or passage applies and it is appropriate to show the practical application of His Word as it applies in a variety of situations.

The wisdom of God says, **"He taught me also, and said unto me, Let thine heart retain my words: keep my commandments, and live."** (Proverbs 4:4)

The Reason for this Volume

To illustrate the need for such Bible based teaching, let's take a look at this email received leading up to the publication of this volume. We assume that this email likely came from a sincere yet deceived person who is seeking the truth. We were glad to receive it and prayerfully speak into this person's life. God bless them richly in Jesus Christ.

Email response to this book title, *I Die Daily*:

> "I wouldn't buy a book that says 'I die daily.' Solutions are needed, not dying. Why buy a book you think is about dying daily and not healing …"

Our response to this email went something like this:

> Hi, and thank you for taking time to comment. In answer to your comment, I would respond this way: According to Christ and His apostles, dying IS the solution, the only solution - that Christ might reign in our bodies and not us - "I am crucified with Christ: nevertheless I live; yet not I, but Christ liveth in me: and the life which I now live in the flesh I live by the faith of the Son of God, who loved me, and gave himself for me." (Gal. 2:20) "He must increase, but I must decrease." (John 3:30) The deceiver (false prophet 'Christian' author) would entice the potential buyer or make merchandise of them (2 Pet. 2:1-3). This he does by alluring them through the lust of the flesh to purchase his book, which is carefully and purposely entitled to attract those looking to salvage what God said must die – the flesh, the old man, sinful nature, the self-will, self-effort, self-aggrandizement, self-esteem, etc. This is why there are titles like – "Best Life Now," and oth-

er reinventing yourself type titles. All these wolves who promise people things that God never promised are set forth by Satan to lead millions astray – and that is what is happening. Their books sell by the millions. The titles and messages are based on the premise of salvaging the sinful or carnal part of us, which Christ and His apostles commanded us to crucify. Paul said that there was "NO good thing" in him except Jesus Christ (Rom. 7:18).

The resurrection life of Christ is only given to those who choose to obey Him by crucifying the deeds of the body and fellowshipping with Him in the fellowship of His sufferings, being made conformable to His death (Luke 22:42; Rom. 6; 8:29; 2 Cor. 4:10-11; Phil. 3:10; etc.).

And yes, laying down your life is what dying daily is – "And he said to them all, If any man will come after me, let him DENY HIMSELF, and take up his cross (implement of death) daily, and follow me. For whosoever will save (love) his life shall lose it: but whosoever will lose his life for my sake, the same shall save it." (Luke 9:23-24)

The "healing" is the resurrection, but it cannot come and will not come until the individual chooses to obey the LORD by daily and experientially dying to self-will and being buried with Christ.

God's blessings to you in Jesus Christ.

As should be obvious to the reader, such a conversation underscores the need for this essential biblical topic to be studied and understood by all who will follow Christ (Hos. 4:6; Matt. 22:29).

Note From the Author

> "For thou art great, and doest wondrous things: thou art God alone. Teach me thy way, O LORD; I will walk in thy truth: unite my heart to fear thy name. I will praise thee, O Lord my God, with all my heart: and I will glorify thy name for evermore. For great is thy mercy toward me: and thou hast delivered my soul from the lowest hell." Psalms 86:10-13

This writer believes there has never been a man more in need of God's all-sufficient grace than this depraved soul whom the LORD has so graciously found, regenerated, and is daily transforming for His holy, eternal purposes (Rom. 6-8; Eph.3:11). He has truly and more than the initial time **"delivered my soul from the lowest hell."** (Ps. 86:13)

> "For we ourselves also were sometimes foolish, disobedient, deceived, serving divers lusts and pleasures, living in malice and envy, hateful, *and* hating one another. But after that the kindness and love of God our Saviour toward man appeared, Not by works of righteousness which we have done, but according to his mercy he saved us, by the washing of regeneration, and renewing of the Holy Ghost; Which he shed on us abundantly through Jesus Christ our Saviour; That being justified by his grace, we should be made heirs according to the hope of eternal life." Titus 3:3-7

All comments concerning this book are welcomed. If anyone can clearly, and through the preponderance of Holy Scripture, demonstrate that anything in this book is not aligned with the mind of Christ as revealed in the full-counsel of His Word, please bring that valid concern to my attention so that correction can be made immediately.

todd@SafeGuardYourSoul.com

This writer has been himself deluded due to lack of knowledge, and wishes to assist others in biblically and spiritually discerning, that they might be spared deception and derailment and fully glorify the LORD who bought them with His precious blood.

> **"Whom having not seen, ye love; in whom, though now ye see *him* not, yet believing, ye rejoice with joy unspeakable and full of glory: Receiving the end of your faith, *even* the salvation of *your* souls." 1 Peter 1:8-9**

His watchmen are to hear and warn.

> **"So thou, O son of man, I have set thee a watchman unto the house of Israel; therefore thou shalt hear the word at my mouth, and warn them from me...Therefore, thou son of man, say unto the children of thy people, The righteousness of the righteous shall not deliver him in the day of his transgression: as for the wickedness of the wicked, he shall not fall thereby in the day that he turneth from his wickedness; neither shall the righteous be able to live for his *righteousness* in the day that he sinneth. When I shall say to the righteous, *that* he shall surely live; if he trust to his own righteousness, and commit iniquity, all his righteousnesses shall not be remembered; but for his iniquity that he hath committed, he shall die for it." Ezekiel 33:7, 12-13**

The LORD told His watchman to **"hear the word at my mouth, and warn them from me."** Like the prophet Ezekiel, the body of Christ is to **"hear"** the Word of God and **"warn"** others of false doctrines which war against revealed truth, corrupting the image and will of the living God in the hearts of men, namely His own people. A **"watchman"** or overseer in the body of Christ is to **"earnestly contend for the faith which was once delivered unto the saints,"** declaring, defending and guarding the divine oracles, and speaking according to them alone (Isa. 8:20; 2 Tim. 4:2-5; 1 Pet. 4:11; Jude 3-4).

The deep concern of this writer and an army of God-fearing men and women, is that without biblical authority, multitudes are being led to believe in a cross-less "Christianity" that is not the original Gospel delivered to us by Christ and His holy apostles. Divine truth protects, and it is our prayer that this volume will be an educational tool for individuals and groups, springboarding each reader into a life of allegiance to Jesus Christ first and foremost. It is also our desire and prayer that each reader would become a doer of divine truth and follow His call to die to self – to be buried deep in the death and burial of Christ – that Jesus Christ might reign supreme in each individual life and among all His saints for whom He shall soon return.

**For the latest resources, please visit
www.SafeGuardYourSoul.com**

Foreword

By Travis Bryan III

This great book focuses in on the most important message to the church today, the cross of Christ and the daily cross for all who will know and follow the LORD. There will never be revival until believers yield and die to self. In these pages, Todd Tomasella shows us the way of the cross, a way which he understands and acknowledges that he himself is daily learning.

One godly reformer referred to the Christian life as a daily baptism, or 'dying upward.' The flesh begins with birth; spirit begins with death. This applies daily, too. The daily door to the Spirit walk is our death with Christ - our daily dying to self (Rom. 8:36; 12:1-2; 1 Cor. 15:31, 36; 2 Cor. 4:10-12). Daily dying is gain (we gain more of Christ). In the last days, men will be lovers of their own selves. We are to hate our old self, not love him (John 12:25). In Galatians 2:20, the Greek verb is in the perfect tense: 'I have been and continue to be crucified with Christ.' The word 'planted' in Romans 6:5 is also in the perfect tense. The Valley of Achor (troubling or horror) is a door of hope (Hos. 2:14-17: Jos. 7:24, 26; Isa. 65:10). To be brought low as in Psalm 116 is to die to self.

The cross is in the Spirit. It is through the Spirit that we are able to MORTIFY (crucify) the sinful deeds of the body (Rom. 8:13; Col. 3:5). Those who belong to Christ have CRUCIFIED the lusts of the flesh (Gal. 5:24).

Table of Contents

CHAPTER ONE
Downward Dying – Upward Rising

CHAPTER TWO
"His Unspeakable Gift"
2 Corinthians 9:15

CHAPTER THREE
The Stone

CHAPTER FOUR
"Raised Up"
2 Corinthians 4:14

CHAPTER FIVE
The Laid Down Life

CHAPTER SIX
"Walk While Ye Have the Light, Lest Darkness Come Upon You"
John 12:35

CHAPTER SEVEN
The Cross, Hearing, & Speaking

CHAPTER EIGHT
The Only Way *Up Is Down*

CHAPTER NINE
"The Gospel which I Preached unto You"
1 Corinthians 15:1

CHAPTER TEN
"Death is Swallowed Up in Victory"
1 Corinthians 15:54

ADDENDUM
Making Peace with God

SafeGuardYourSoul.com

Chapter One

Downward Dying—Upward Rising

"And the remnant that is escaped of the house of Judah shall again take root downward, and bear fruit upward." Isaiah 37:31

The Rhythm of the Gospel

The rhythm of the Gospel is down – up, down – up, down – up. Jesus went down in His earthly life, then up on that cross, then down in that grave, then upward in resurrection into Heaven. Though at the moment He sits on high, soon He will descend downward as He returns for His beloved people.

God's aim is that His Son will be glorified to raise up His people, and yet He will not do such until the individual disciple takes **"root downward."** (Isa. 37:31) This involves personal agreement and participation in losing our lives in Christ that we might find them (Jn. 12:24-25).

It's only the bowed down remnant of Christ's kingdom that He will raise up to fruitfulness and eternal glory with Him. Living the **"raised up"** life consists of laying down flat before the LORD in utter humility before His Majesty – taking **"root downward"** so He can then cause you to **"bear fruit upward."** (Isa. 37:31)

Jesus taught us that only the seeds that fall into the ground and die are going to bring forth fruit unto eternal life for God's eternal glory (Jn. 12:24). Our hearts and minds must be permeated with this truth that is central to the Gospel message. May God bless us to **"receive with meekness the engrafted word, which is able to save (y)our souls"** as we take in, meditate upon, and obey our LORD's message of the cross (Lk. 9:23-24; James 1:21). This volume is designed to do just that – impress and invest this message deep into the heart of the saint.

The downward bowing saint is perpetually upheld by His free Spirit (Ps. 51:12). As we are **"Always bearing about in the body the dying of the Lord Jesus,"** His resurrection life is propelling us upward (Jn. 11:25; 2 Cor. 4:10). The crucified disciple, by the divine power of Jesus Christ working in him, is moved forward and upward into blessed fruitfulness to Heaven's glory. As the cross is taken up, **"the life also of Jesus"** is **"made manifest in our body."**

> **"Always bearing about in the body the dying of the Lord Jesus, that the life also of Jesus might be made manifest in our body. For we which live are alway delivered unto death for Jesus' sake, that the life also of Jesus might be made manifest in our mortal flesh. So then death worketh in us, but life in you ... Knowing that**

> **he which raised up the Lord Jesus shall raise up us also by Jesus, and shall present us with you." 2 Corinthians 4:10-14**

The early apostles had the life of Jesus in them, which was evident to all who ever came into their presence. They didn't have seminary degrees, nor were they educated men, but were wholly given over to the LORD Jesus. Observe with me what the Holy Ghost-inspired writer pens in Acts about what others witnessed concerning Peter and John:

> **"Now when they saw the boldness of Peter and John, and perceived that they were unlearned and ignorant men, they marvelled; and <u>they took knowledge of them, that they had been with Jesus</u>." Acts 4:13**

An undeniable and **"notable miracle"** had just been done by the power of God working in these men; look at what the Bible says concerning how the power of Jesus impacted their world:

> **"Saying, What shall we do to these men? for that indeed a notable miracle hath been done by them is manifest to all them that dwell in Jerusalem; and we cannot deny it." Acts 4:16**

There is no shortcut – **"So then death worketh in us, but life in you."** (2 Cor. 4:12) It is only as we are being ushered into His holy presence in daily communion with Him, that His divine life swallows up and consumes us. The Holy Spirit is then working in our vessels to suppress and crucify sin and self, and bring glory to Jesus Christ (Rom. 8:13-14; 2 Cor. 3:18; Gal. 2:20; 6:14). By His blessed power, we are then made able to accomplish anything and all He leads us into. We are *then* equipped by Him, not *before*. Paul the apostle prayed:

> **"That he would grant you, according to the riches of his glory, to be strengthened with might by his Spirit in the inner man ... Now unto him that is able to do exceeding abundantly above all that we ask or think, according to the power that worketh in us." Ephesians 3:16, 20**

As death works in us by the daily cross, His divine life empowers us and bellows out of us, working for His glory in and through our vessels.

Any person who is walking in the Holy Spirit is dying downward and being simultaneously lifted upward by the resurrecting divine power. He is fruitful and blessed; his leaf shall not wither (Ps. 1:3; Jer. 17:5-9). There can and will be no resurrection life working in me unless there is first the killing power of the cross in me; then when there is that downward dying, there is simultaneously that upward raising by His Holy Ghost, raising up this vessel to His glory.

> **"Knowing that he which raised up the Lord Jesus shall raise up us also by Jesus, and shall present us with you." 2 Corinthians 4:10**

The divine muscle of the cross cannot be overestimated. The power of the embraced cross and the consequential raising up by the Holy Spirit, is inestimable in value. All aspects of the cross should be considered, beginning with the redeeming blood of Christ's cross.

> "What does this mean for us? Remember that there are two aspects of Christ's death. He died for our sins. He died for us – substitution. But then Paul tells us that we are also to die with Him. 'I have been crucified WITH CHRIST' (Gal. 2:20): 'Reckon ye also yourselves to be dead indeed unto sin' (Rom. 6:11). The Israelites in bondage were delivered by the blood shed and sprinkled. But they

> are pursued by certain of their foes. These foes are slain at the Red Sea, but they themselves escape and are free. Egypt stands for the world of sin. Christ found us in 'Egypt,' and by His death in our stead delivered us from the penalty of sin. But even after our conversion some of these sins followed us and harassed us – temper, pride, jealousy, lust, worry, avarice – causing discomfiture and misery, and occasionally temporary defeat. Where is there any escape, any real victory? Only through the Red Sea – baptism, or what baptism implies; i.e., a death to sin and a rising again to righteousness. That is a crucifixion with Christ, so as to be able to 'reckon ourselves dead indeed unto sin.'" *How to Live the Victorious Life*, by an Unknown Christian

The believer's cross – as taken up in obedience to the crucified Savior – is that cross that separates us from the world, the fleshly self, and those who are perishing (Rom. 1:16; 6:7; 1 Cor. 1:18; Gal. 2:20; 6:14; Col. 1:14, 20). The cross is the answer and solution to all of man's problems, not self-help programs or books, seminars, conferences, seminary, 12-step programs, or any other counterfeit.

> "I, like other believers, have tasted the resurrection blessing after a dying to self. Once you taste it, it becomes easier the next time. It's not a formula that always works (we should never think we can put God in a box), but it is God's program for today. The cross has replaced the law (Gal. 3:1-3; 2:19-21). Only the cross can stamp out self. Every other program ends up in licentiousness (license for sin) or legalism." Travis Bryan III

"A Tree Planted by the Waters"
Jeremiah 17:7

Observe in Jeremiah 17 the fruitfulness of that trusting disciple who is planted down deep into the soil of the LORD:

> **"Blessed is the man that trusteth in the LORD, and whose hope the LORD is. For he shall be as a tree planted by the waters, and that spreadeth out her roots by the river, and shall not see when heat cometh, but her leaf shall be green; and shall not be careful in the year of drought, neither shall cease from yielding fruit." Jeremiah 17:7-8**

"A tree planted by the waters" goes down deep into the earth and receives simultaneous watering, and is thereby raised up into great fruitfulness. This is a picture of what the LORD intends for each of us. Are you ready to sink down and die deep so that He might raise you high in His power and for His blessed glory?

Those who walk according to another gospel – one that is cross-less – are bound in deception and bound for eternal damnation. They are not being **"raised up"** by the same Holy Spirit that raised Christ from the dead, because He simply will not raise up any vessel that is still alive under its own power. He only raises up those that are bowed down in humility before Him and crucified with Christ (Ps. 145:14; Gal. 2:20). **"The counsel of the ungodly"** would deceive us into skirting the essential cross and doing things in our own feeble and foolish wisdom. With this in mind, let's prayerfully and carefully read the first Psalm.

Psalms 1:

> "Blessed is the man that walketh not in the counsel of the ungodly, nor standeth in the way of sinners, nor sitteth in the seat of the scornful. But his delight is in the law of the LORD; and in his law doth he meditate day and night. And he shall be like a tree planted by the rivers of water, that bringeth forth his fruit in his season; his leaf also shall not wither; and whatsoever he doeth shall prosper. The ungodly are not so: but are like the chaff which the wind driveth away. Therefore the ungodly shall not stand in the judgment, nor sinners in the congregation of the righteous. For the LORD knoweth the way of the righteous: but the way of the ungodly shall perish."

The grace, peace, truth, love and fruitfulness of our God abound to each of God's people this day and hour. The LORD bless and enable each of us to be conformed to the crucified image of Jesus Christ as we expect the soon return of our blessed LORD and Savior (Rom. 8:29; Gal. 2:20).

To all those who are cheerfully giving themselves over to the LORD – who are being crucified with Christ – the exceeding great and precious promise of the LORD is as such:

> "And God is able to make all grace abound toward you; that ye, always having all sufficiency in all things, may abound to every good work."
> **2 Corinthians 9:8**

It is the Holy Spirit of God who allows us to be brought to the revelation and realization of our own complete hopelessness and inability to be right or do right with His enabling grace. He brings us to this place so **"that**

the power of Christ may rest upon" us. In our own **"weakness"** and our own **"infirmities,"** as we are crucified with Him, His sufficiency and power rests upon us.

> **"And he said unto me, My grace is sufficient for thee: for my strength is made perfect in weakness. Most gladly therefore will I rather glory in my infirmities, that the power of Christ may rest upon me." 2 Corinthians 12:9**

Jesus Christ is the very power and wisdom of God. He who is all in all has been made toward us wisdom and power personified.

> **"But unto them which are called, both Jews and Greeks, Christ the power of God, and the wisdom of God." 1 Corinthians 1:24**

PRAYER: *Heavenly Father, thank You for Your perfect plan, revealed so clearly in Your Holy Word. At this very moment, if never before, I bow down before You, and ask You to bless my desire to be Yours. Grant repentance where needed and take over my whole vessel. I now yield full control and reign in my life to You. I bow down deeply and beg You to enable me to die deeply, that You might fully possess and raise this life up to bring Your glory alone! Amen.*

Capture Points

- *Write out Isaiah 37:31 on an index card (with reference). Meditate upon it and memorize it as you carry it with you (KJV recommended).*

- *Worshipfully discuss the biblical dynamics of 2 Corinthians 4:10-14.*

- *Read Psalms 1.*

Chapter Two

His Unspeakable Gift
2 Corinthians 9:15

"Thanks be unto God for his unspeakable gift" 2 Corinthians 9:15

Because of the **"unspeakable gift"** of our redemption in Christ, we can now richly receive and drink in the infinite wonders of the goodness of God every day, as those *raised up* from out of that state of death we inherited from Adam (Rom. 5:12). Truly He **"giveth us richly all things to enjoy"**, and for that we are forever grateful! (1 Tim. 6:17)

> **"O the depth of the riches both of the wisdom and knowledge of God! how unsearchable are his judgments, and his ways past finding out!" Romans 11:33**

Due to the bountiful beauty of the LORD and how He has shown such mercy on us, we should let our joyful hearts praise and magnify Him with reckless abandon (Heb. 13:15).

That we may experience and be grateful for His **"unspeakable gift"** of Christ and His salvation, may the LORD bless each of us to be possessed with the revelation of our need to sink down deep into His death and burial, that He might raise us up in His glory! *Positionally*, we are already there, yet we must *experience* the cross daily by setting aside our own will and person in gratitude and obedience, in preference of His divine Person and will reigning in us. He has ordained that we **"reign in life by one, Jesus Christ."**

We are born in Adam and reborn in Christ to reign in this life by His infinite power and grace.

> **"For if by one man's (Adam's) offence death reigned by one; much more they which receive abundance of grace and of the gift of righteousness shall reign in life by one, Jesus Christ.)" Romans 5:17**

Exploring in Holy Writ and getting a glimpse of the sin from which we have been saved and the eternal consequences of that sin, we who have been brought back into relationship with God must choose daily to keep crucified that sinful nature from which He rescued us. God is **"Holy, holy, holy"** and sin defiles men in His holy sight (Isa. 6:3; Mk. 7:20-23; Rev. 4:8). But sin is more than just an act – it is a state of the heart if allowed. With this in mind and at heart, may God bless each of us to fear Him and to **"work out"** our **"own salvation with fear and trembling,"** never taking for granted His free gift of grace and vainly acting as if we were granted a license for sin (Rom. 6:1-2, 15; Phil. 2:12; Heb. 12:14-15; Jude 3-4).

> **"And they that are Christ's have crucified the**

> flesh with the affections and lusts." Galatians 5:24

> "But <u>we had the sentence of death in ourselves</u>, that we should not trust in ourselves, but in God which raiseth the dead." 2 Corinthians 1:9

The "Resurrection of Life" or the "Resurrection of Damnation"?

> "Unto you first God, having <u>raised up</u> his Son Jesus, sent him to bless you, in turning away every one of you from his iniquities." Acts 3:26

He told us that those who bow will be raised, right? Those who, at His blessed beckoning, bow in humility and repentance are gloriously saved by Him. We will therefore be *raised up* to everlasting life with Him in the **"resurrection of life,"** instead of the **"resurrection of damnation."** (Jn. 5:29)

Every one of us is going to be *raised up* – either to **"life"** or to **"damnation."**

> "Marvel not at this: for the hour is coming, in the which all that are in the graves shall hear his voice, And shall come forth; they that have done good, unto the resurrection of life; and they that have done evil, unto the resurrection of damnation." John 5:28-29

Christ told us this about Himself, which we also need to emulate: **"I can of mine own self do nothing: as I hear, I judge: and my judgment is just; because I seek not mine own will, but the will of the Father which hath sent me."** (Jn. 5:30) This is our *experiential* cross to be daily taken up (Matt. 16:24-26; Lk. 9:23-24). Now if the Son of God could do **"nothing"** by His **"own self,"** how can we expect to do such?

It is in bowing down humbly before His Majesty that one will be **"raised up"** by Him in the next life, and also presently **"raised up"** into a life well pleasing to Him, with power and grace in Jesus Christ.

It is very important to realize our place with God and how that it was purchased for us by Jesus Christ, without whom we are utterly without hope.

> **"To wit, that God was in Christ, reconciling the world unto himself, not imputing their trespasses unto them; and hath committed unto us the word of reconciliation." 2 Corinthians 5:19**

The LORD has brought us *out* of something and *into* something else. What is that something else? Are you on a quest to investigate the wonders of His love and the salvation He wrought for you? (See Deut. 6:22-25; Eph. 2:1-10; Col. 1:12-14; Heb. 2:3.)

Together, let's pore over a grand passage in Romans 3:

> **"For <u>all have sinned</u>, and come short of the glory of God; Being justified freely by his grace through the redemption that is in Christ Jesus: Whom God hath set forth to be a propitiation through faith in his blood, to declare his righteousness for the remission of sins that are past, through the forbearance of God; To declare, I say, at this time his righteousness: that he might be just, and the justifier of him which believeth in Jesus. Where is boasting then? It is excluded. By what law? of works? Nay: but by the law of faith. Therefore we conclude that a man is justified by faith without the deeds of the law." vv. 23-28**

No man deserves God's redemption and forgiveness. It can only be received as a free gift. This happens when one is brought to repentance for his sins and makes the choice to receive Christ and His pardon (Jn. 1:12; Acts 2:38; 3:19; 20:21).

> **"For who maketh thee to differ from another? and <u>what hast thou that thou didst not receive? now if thou didst receive it, why dost thou glory, as if thou hadst not received it?</u>" 1 Corinthians 4:7**

The recipient of His salvation has nothing to glory in as concerns self. We all have sinned against the LORD grossly and deserve and merit eternal punishment for our transgressions. We have only to boast in Jesus Christ – the true identity of all who are Heaven bound. Christ bought our salvation with His own precious blood.

> **"Forasmuch as ye know that ye were not redeemed with corruptible things, as silver and gold, from your vain conversation received by tradition from your fathers; But with the precious blood of Christ, as of a lamb without blemish and without spot." 1 Peter 1:18-19**

Not one of us is even capable of finding God. He who paid for all our sins in His own blood found us (Jn. 3:27; 6:44; 1 Jn. 4:9-10; 19).

> **"Behold, what manner of love the Father hath bestowed upon us, that we should be called the sons of God: therefore the world knoweth us not, because it knew him not." 1 John 3:1**

What have we to die to? We must understand the true state from which we have been rescued, and the "**so great salvation**" into which we have been purchased by "**the blood of his cross**." (Col. 1:20; Heb. 2:3)

This includes the revelation that all our own

"righteousnesses are as filthy rags," and that it is **"not by works of righteousness which we have done,"** but rather that Christ, who was sinless, became sin for us that we might be made the righteousness of God in Him (Isa. 64:6; 2 Cor. 5:21).

> **"Not by works of righteousness which we have done, but according to his mercy he saved us, by the washing of regeneration, and renewing of the Holy Ghost; Which he shed on us abundantly through Jesus Christ our Saviour; That being justified by his grace, we should be made heirs according to the hope of eternal life." Titus 3:5-7**

He who knew no sin, and was harmless and completely innocent, died in our place. He took the blow of death for us – to bring us to God and to make us new creatures in Him, forgiving all sin and enabling us to live pleasing to Him in all things.

> **"For he hath made him to be sin for us, who knew no sin; that we might be made the righteousness of God in him." 2 Corinthians 5:21**

Through Christ's perfect sacrifice and the gift of His salvation, God **"hath raised us up (positionally) together, and made us sit together in heavenly places in Christ Jesus."** Why? **"That in the ages to come he might shew the exceeding riches of his grace in his kindness toward us through Christ Jesus."** (Eph. 2:6-7)

How do we receive such an **"unspeakable gift"?** (2 Cor. 9:15) **"For by grace are ye saved through faith; and that not of yourselves: it is the gift of God: Not of works, lest any man should boast."** (Eph. 2:8-9)

Not one of us deserves or merits God's pardon for our myriad of evil deeds and depravity (Gen. 6:5, 12; Jer.

17:9; Rom. 3:23; 6:23). This is why each of us should stop right here and now and rejoice with Paul in saying, **"Thanks be unto God for his unspeakable gift."** (2 Cor. 9:15)

One thing is certain – Jesus Christ is the only Savior. Any person who denies this truth calls the Son of God a liar (Jn. 3:14-16; 5:23; 14:6; Acts 4:12; 1 Tim. 2:5; 1 Jn. 5:1-12; Rev. 1:8).

The follower of Christ must understand that Christ alone is his righteousness, and he must die to his own righteousness and any attempt to somehow merit the acceptance Jesus already earned for us. He was the only One qualified, and He perfectly accomplished His mission. All self-dependence and self-righteousness must be crucified. Paul, the servant of Christ, cried:

> **"And be found in him, not having mine own righteousness, which is of the law, but that which is through the faith of Christ, the righteousness which is of God by faith. That I may know him, and the power of his resurrection, and the fellowship of his sufferings, being made conformable unto his death." Philippians 3:9-10**

If we will be **"found in him,"** we must denounce all self-righteousness in order to be clothed in His righteousness. In order to **"know him,"** I must be *raised up* in **"the power of his resurrection,"** and to do this I must experience **"the fellowship of his sufferings, being made conformable unto his death."** Such a statement and many others in Holy Scripture would be completely unnecessary if there were no danger of forfeiting one's place with God (see Ezek. 33:12-13; 2 Pet. 2:20-21).

If one's spiritual state of **"righteousness"** (right standing with God) was automatically and unalterably fixed after he was initially saved, why then would the apostle Paul be concerned about being **"found in him, not having mine own righteousness"**? (To further research this important subject, see the book titled *Lie of the Ages* at www.SafeGuardYourSoul.com)

> **"When I shall say to the righteous, that he shall surely live; if he trust to his own righteousness, and commit iniquity, all his righteousnesses shall not be remembered; but for his iniquity that he hath committed, he shall die for it." Ezekiel 33:13**

All our attempts to merit God's favor, redemption, or forgiveness are futile – before and after we are initially saved. If we could do such, God would never have sent His only begotten Son to die in our place (Gal. 2:21).

> **"But we are all as an unclean thing, and all our righteousnesses are as filthy rags; and we all do fade as a leaf; and our iniquities, like the wind, have taken us away." Isaiah 64:6**

It would behoove us to embrace this simple truth. Christ alone is our righteousness. He alone atoned for our sins when we were otherwise hopeless and helpless to get back to our Maker, due to Adam's sin and the consequent death that passed upon all men after him (Rom. 5:12).

Concerning this last hour and being found in His righteousness and not our own (which is useless), Jesus said:

> **"He that overcometh, the same shall be clothed in white raiment; and I will not blot out his name out of the book of life, but I will confess his name before my Father, and before his angels." Revelation 3:5**

Are you beginning to see why the Holy Ghost moved through Paul to speak of the danger of being found having his **"own righteousness"?** (Phil. 3:9) Those who overcome through Christ's grace and their own obedience to Him, will be found in Him and pleasing to God. All others will be outside of His eternal kingdom (Rev. 21:8, 27; 22:15). These overcomers will be raised up in this life to please and be fruitful to Him, and also to reign with Him in the next life.

PRAYER: *Father, thank You so much for the unspeakable gift of salvation You purchased for me by the precious blood of Christ Jesus, my LORD and Savior. I love You, Jesus, and thank You so much for shedding Your holy, sinless blood for me on the cross. Bless me to lay down my life in this world that You might raise me up to bear fruit to Your glory. Amen.*

Capture Points

- What is the **"unspeakable gift"** of God? 2 Corinthians 9:15.

- In a Spirit-led, God-fearing posture, prayerfully and biblically contrast one's own righteousness with God's righteousness, as seen in the following passages: Isaiah 64:6; Romans 3:21-26; 2 Corinthians 5:21. Feel free to introduce other pertinent passages from God's Word.

- Discuss Revelation 3:5.

SafeGuardYourSoul.com

Chapter Three

The Stone
Top or Bottom

"And whosoever shall fall on this stone shall be broken: but on whomsoever it shall fall, it will grind him to powder." Matthew 21:44

If I am following the Master, I am becoming more and more of a servant as He was. When He promotes me, it is for the purpose of serving Him and His people in a greater fashion, not so I can be exalted in the sight of men (Ps. 75:5-6). If I am to **"grow in grace,"** it is in order that I may know and love Him more and serve His people more fully (2 Pet. 1:2; 3:18).

This short life is not the occasion to be exalted among men, but rather to exalt the only One worthy to be exalted.

> **"And I, if I be lifted up from the earth, will draw all men unto me." John 12:32**

Yes, I know He is speaking of His own death to save us, and yet I must take liberty to ask: Are we lifting Him up? One of the clearest ways we lift up the Savior is to lift up His will, which is His Word, by doing it. In this and through this, men will see His goodness in you and glorify your Father in Heaven (Matt. 5:16).

Where are my motives in serving God? Why do I want to be in leadership in the Body of Christ? Why do I want to sing in the choir, preach, teach Sunday School, greet, write a book, have a ministry, etc.? Is it to be seen of men like the religious hypocrites of Christ's day, or is it to lift up the downtrodden, see God heal the brokenhearted, give hope to the hopeless, and exalt the King of all kings? Is this not why Christ came? (Luke 4:18; Jn. 12:32; Col. 1:17-19)

Christ is to be magnified in all things in the lives of those whom He has redeemed:

> **"Christ shall be magnified in my body, whether it be by life, or by death." Philippians 1:20**

Please read the following words carefully and prayerfully. These are not the words of any mere man. These are the words of the Alpha and the Omega, the One who spoke the worlds into existence and now upholds them by the very word He spoke when He created all things. Jesus Christ is the One who created, sustains, and owns all things, yet came to this earth to serve us (John 1:10). The text below is paramount to understanding and walking in your God-given purpose in this life, as you follow Christ in what He did in His time here on the earth, as He showed us the Father (Jn. 14:9).

> "Then came to him the mother of Zebedee's children with her sons, worshipping him, and desiring a certain thing of him. And he said unto her, What wilt thou? She saith unto him, Grant that these my two sons may sit, the one on thy right hand, and the other on the left, in thy kingdom. But Jesus answered and said, Ye know not what ye ask. Are ye able to drink of the cup that I shall drink of, and to be baptized with the baptism that I am baptized with? They say unto him, We are able. And he saith unto them, Ye shall drink indeed of my cup, and be baptized with the baptism that I am baptized with: but to sit on my right hand, and on my left, is not mine to give, but it shall be given to them for whom it is prepared of my Father. And when the ten heard it, they were moved with indignation against the two brethren. But Jesus called them unto him, and said, Ye know that the princes of the Gentiles exercise dominion over them, and they that are great exercise authority upon them. But it shall not be so among you: but whosoever will be great among you, let him be your minister; And whosoever will be chief among you, let him be your servant: Even as the Son of man came not to be ministered unto, but to minister, and to give his life a ransom for many." Matthew 20:20-28

Jesus came to serve us and commanded us to do what He did – serve others.

> "Let nothing be done through strife or vainglory; but in lowliness of mind let each esteem other better than themselves. Look not every man on his own things, but every man also on the things of others. Let this mind be in you, which was also in Christ Jesus." Philippians 2:3

-5

Who Do We Think We Are?

If you have anything good about you at all, God is to be blamed (Rom. 3:10; 7:18). Every good and perfect gift originates from Him, and not from us (James 1:17). We have no existence without Him who is our life.

Take a look at what Paul says about the giftings we have all been given on loan:

> **"For who maketh thee to differ from another? and what hast thou that thou didst not receive? now if thou didst receive it, why dost thou glory (boast), as if thou hadst not received it?" 1 Corinthians 4:7**

If we have been given something, that means it didn't originate with us. Right? It also means that God gave the gift(s) to us to serve others, not just ourselves (1 Pet. 4:10-11), so why do we arrogantly boast in our hearts as if we are better than others because of something God Himself gave us? Rather we should be using those gifts to serve His people (1 Peter 4:10-11).

Here are the 3 questions the great apostle poses here in 1 Corinthians 4:7:

- **"For who maketh thee to differ from another?"**

- **"What hast thou that thou didst not receive?"**

  "If thou didst receive it, why dost thou glory (boast), as if thou hadst not received it?"

We don't own the giftings resident in our lives. These inherent gifts are merely on loan to us from the LORD. Each of us is responsible to God for the stewardship of these tools of service, and will one day give account for how we chose to use them. Am I using them to serve Him and His people, or am I utilizing His gifts in me to glorify my own name?

> "As every man hath received the gift, even so minister (use in service) the same one to another, as good stewards of the manifold grace of God. If any man speak, let him speak as the oracles of God; if any man minister, let him do it as of the ability which God giveth: <u>that God in all things may be glorified through Jesus Christ, to whom be praise and dominion for ever and ever. Amen</u>." 1 Peter 4:10-11

The crucified life will bring about the producing of His good fruit in us, and the fruitful use of the gifts He placed in each of us (Rom. 1:11; Phil. 2:3-5).

More questions from God:

> "Shall the ax boast itself against him that heweth therewith? or shall the saw magnify itself against him that shaketh it? as if the rod should shake itself against them that lift it up, or as if the staff should lift up itself, as if it were no wood." Isaiah 10:15

God Hates Arrogance

> "Talk no more so exceeding proudly; let not arrogancy come out of your mouth: for the LORD is a God of knowledge, and by him actions are weighed." 1 Samuel 2:3

> "The fear of the LORD is to hate evil: pride, and arrogancy, and the evil way, and the froward mouth, do I hate." Proverbs 8:13

> "And I will punish the world for their evil, and the wicked for their iniquity; and I will cause

> the arrogancy of the proud to cease, and will lay low the haughtiness of the terrible." Isaiah 13:11

It is abundantly clear in the aforementioned verses of Scripture that the LORD will humble those who refuse to humble themselves. He also stated:

> "But he giveth more grace. Wherefore he saith, God resisteth (sets Himself against) the proud, but giveth grace unto the humble." James 4:6

The prideful heart is a deceived heart:

> "For if a man think himself to be something, when he is nothing, he deceiveth himself." Galatians 6:3

The Cure for Arrogance

> "For I say, through the grace given unto me, to every man that is among you, not to think of himself more highly than he ought to think; but to think soberly, according as God hath dealt to every man the measure of faith." Romans 12:3

> "He hath showed thee, O man, what is good; and what doth the LORD require of thee, but to do justly, and to love mercy, and to walk humbly with thy God?" Micah 6:8

> "He must increase, but I must decrease." John 3:30

Oh, that God would place in us the fleshly heart of a true servant who serves Him and others regardless of whether or not any man is looking, or whether he receives any reward on this earth.

Your Predestination

> "For whom he did foreknow, he also did predestinate to be conformed to the image of his Son, that he might be the firstborn among many brethren." Romans 8:29

God did **"predestinate us to be conformed to the image of his Son."** You might respond to this Scriptural truth by asking, "Okay, what does it mean to be conformed to the image of Jesus Christ, the Son of God?" Here is God's answer:

> **"Let this mind be in you, which was also in Christ Jesus: Who, being in the form of God, thought it not robbery to be equal with God: But made himself of no reputation, and took upon him the form of a <u>servant</u>, and was made in the likeness of men: And being found in fashion as a man, he humbled himself, and became obedient unto death, even the death of the cross." Philippians 2:5-8**

In order for the cross to have its full effect in my life, mine must be a self-emptying life that is submissive and obedient to God's commands (Isa. 1:19-20; Jn. 14:15. 21-23; 1 Jn. 2:3-6). Those who have emptied themselves of the self-life are blessed to have willing and obedient hearts. They have given over the right to their own life and will to Christ (Jn. 12:24-25). They do not attempt to make up their own rules, because they are not existing under their own rule and power, but are rather emptied of self so that they are free to worship and serve Him **"in spirit and in truth."** (Jn. 4:23-24)

In the Father's infinite wisdom and love, He sent **"His only begotten Son,"** who emptied Himself – divested Himself – and left the glory of Heaven to be born of a virgin (Jn. 1:14). Jesus came to die (Jn. 12:23-33; Rom.

14:9; 1 Jn. 3:8). Have you owned this mission as your own – to die that He might live and reign in your mortal body?

How rooted am I in Christ? How deep am I planted in His death? The root or depth of root, determines the fruit (Isa. 37:31; Rom. 11:6).

> "A man really believes not what he recites in his creed, but only the things he is ready to die for." Richard Wurmbrand

If you will stop and consider just how different your personal Christianity may be from that of early believers, you may find that your relationship and commitment to Jesus Christ is shallow rooted and incomplete, and that you have not decided to live and die as they did – that you have been unwilling to love not your own life even unto death (Rev. 12:11). In the sentencing of yourself to the complete covering and whelming of the tomb of death, you will discover His life raising you upward, and thereafter your heart will be unwilling to deny Him.

Many who at initial salvation stood broken and repentant before that cross of Christ, have never since experienced the power of that cross – to slay their old man and allow the divine raising up of their lives in glory to God. That cross from which His crimson and cleansing blood flowed so freely, is the redeeming cross of His love both initially and perpetually. He cannot raise up that which has not first been slain in voluntary death and burial. The Gospel is not complete without first a death and burial, then a resurrection.

> "Before the cross of Christ countless men and women of every generation and culture have stood in adoring wonder and humble penitence. The cross stands at the very heart of the Christian faith, manifesting the love of God, effecting salva-

tion from sin, conquering the hostile forces of evil and inviting reconciliation with God." Derek Tidball, *The Message of the Cross*

In the days of His flesh, Christ honored and served His Father and then **"became obedient unto death, even the death of the cross."** (Phil. 2:8) The Father sent the Son and the Son sent the Holy Ghost, who now leads and empowers His people whom He has sent (Matt. 28:18-20; Mk. 16:15-20). The divine Person of the Holy Spirit anoints and enables the death and burial of the saints of God (Rom. 8:13). His disciples follow Him – by becoming obedient unto the death of their own will and desires that they might glorify Him in all things, just as He did concerning His Father. This is what the cross is – a laying down of one's own will for the LORD's. It boils down to who it is we love most.

Unlike Christ, many today want to be somebody who is known and elevated among men in this brief life.

> **"For they loved the praise of men more than the praise of God." John 12:43**

Some of those in places of leadership today act as if they are God's gift to the world instead of possessing the heart posture of a humble servant. They are not dead to self, and are therefore not **"alive unto God through Jesus Christ our Lord."** (Rom. 6:11) These are those **"whose god is their belly (sinful appetites)."** (Phil. 3:17-21) They are **"enemies of the cross of Christ"** - they are not dying to the sinful nature, and consequently desire to be exalted amidst God's people. Many in leadership make a **"vain show"** or **"fair show in the flesh"**. (Ps. 39:5-6; Gal. 6:12) They reign as kings in the midst of the people. These serve themselves as they build their own kingdoms upon the sand foundation of depraved and finite self, and miss the unspeakable joy and opportunity to build upon the Rock of salvation Himself, the only real and eternal **"foundation...which is Jesus Christ."** (1 Cor. 3:11) In doing this, they are leading **"many"** astray, as Christ promised the **"false prophets"** would do in the last days (Matt. 25:3-5; 11, 24).

In stark contrast to those who seek their own glory, the very Creator and King of all kings Himself came to earth and **"made himself of no reputation, and took upon him the form of a servant."** (Phil. 2:7)

Serving self in the midst of a ministry leadership role can be so very subtle. Most who engage in such don't even realize it because the sin of pride and arrogancy blinds the heart and mind (Heb. 3:13). They are fully responsible for this sin because God commands all who will be His to humble themselves in His holy sight.

Overseers have the responsibility of being servant-leaders among God's people. This is their calling:

> **"The elders which are among you I exhort, who am also an elder, and a witness of the sufferings of Christ, and also a partaker of the glory that shall be revealed: Feed the flock of God which is among you, taking the oversight thereof, not by constraint, but willingly; not for filthy lucre, but of a ready mind; <u>Neither as being lords over God's heritage</u>, but being ensamples to the flock. And when the chief Shepherd shall appear, ye shall receive a crown of glory that fadeth not away." 1 Peter 5:1-4**

Friend, where are we allowing ourselves to be led? The Word tells us that **"the leaders of this people cause them to err; and they that are led of them are destroyed."** (Isa. 9:16) We are also warned not to be **"led away with the error of the wicked."** (2 Pet. 3:17) Just as Jesus and His holy apostles and prophets foretold, blind leaders are leading to damnation millions who believe they are following Christ (Matt. 24:3-5, 11, 24; 1 Tim. 4:1-3; 2 Tim. 3:13; 4:2-5; 1 Jn. 4:1-3).

There are several people revealed in the Bible who started off right in their leadership calling, yet ended up destroyed. These were apostates. Remember Saul, Lot's wife, and Judas? These all had one thing in common – pride, rebellion, and arrogance. These were people who were in God's grace, and anointed for leadership by Him, but refused to remain humbled before His presence. This tragedy is the same thing we see happening today among many who now occupy leadership positions within the visible church world at large. They hold and have remained in leadership positions, even while they have departed **"from the faith."** (1 Tim. 4:1-3) The Bible foretold that in the final days some would **"depart from the faith,"** not the pulpit (1 Tim. 4:1-3).

According to the Holy Spirit speaking through the apostle Paul, one must **"keep under"** his body – the sinful nature – if he will prevent becoming ultimately **"castaway"** from the LORD eternally (1 Cor. 9:27).

The Stone

Will you choose to fall upon Him and be broken and blessed? Or will the stone of His judgment crush you in the end?

> **"And whosoever shall fall on this stone shall be broken: but on whomsoever it shall fall, it will grind him to powder." Matthew 21:44**

Did you catch that?! Will you humble yourself, or will God have to humble you eternally by confining your conscious soul to hell? Will you be voluntarily broken before God, or in judgment be crushed to fine powder (destroyed)? God never fails - the choice lies in the individual (Lk. 21:19, 34-36; 2 Tim. 2:11-13). One will choose to willingly and obediently fall upon the Rock of all ages and be broken, or he will soon be crushed to powder by the Lion of Judah in His retribution of all rebellious souls (Amos 9:10; Isa. 1:19-20; 2 Thess. 1:7-10; Rev. 19:12-16).

> **"Humble yourselves in the sight of the Lord, and he shall lift you up." James 4:10**

Prayer for the Humility of Christ

O Father, please remove every trace of self-glorification and arrogance from my being. Let not my left hand know what my right hand is doing. This moment I choose to humble myself under Your mighty hand and to realize I am nothing and can do nothing without You, Jesus. LORD, thank You for Your example. Please teach me to know You in true humility as I serve Your precious people and the lost souls You were crucified to save. LORD, I now present my body a living sacrifice to Thee. Please grant my heart to be established by Your grace and an inspired humility, that I may be well pleasing in Thy holy sight this day. In Jesus' name. Amen.

Capture Points

- Discuss the central truth behind the words of our LORD recorded in Matthew 21:44. Begin with how this truth pertained to Christ, and conclude with how it pertains to us daily.

- On an index card, print out (hand written) Philippians 1:20 so as to be able to begin to assimilate, meditate upon, and memorize this divine truth (KJV recommended).

- Transcribe on an index card the words of John the Baptist found in John 3:30.

Chapter Four

"Raised Up"

"Knowing that he which <u>raised up</u> the Lord Jesus shall <u>raise up</u> us also by Jesus, and shall present us with you." 2 Corinthians 4:14

In the context of this passage, the Holy Spirit is speaking through His servant Paul to those who are **"Always bearing about in the body the dying of the Lord Jesus."** The promise of being **"raised up"** in verse 14 (above) is to those whose lives are **"dead"** and who are therefore **"hid with Christ in God."** (Col. 3:3) The **"remnant"** are specifically identified in that they have sentenced the self-life to death and **"have crucified the flesh with the affections and lusts."** (Isa. 37:31; 2 Cor. 1:19; Gal. 5:24) They are dying downward as God raises them upward in His holy power. Here are the inspired words that precede the verse above:

> "Always bearing about in the body the dying of the Lord Jesus, that the life also of Jesus might be made manifest in our body. For we which live are alway delivered unto death for Jesus' sake, that the life also of Jesus might be made manifest in our mortal flesh. So then death worketh in us, but life in you." 2 Corinthians 4:10-12

The phrase **"raised up"** appears 46 times in Holy Scripture. So that we begin to be infused with the divine rhythm and sequence of the true Gospel (death, burial, resurrection), let us look at some of the verses in which we find the phrase **"raised up,"** also keeping in mind that God never raises something that isn't first dead and buried.

> "Thou fool, that which thou sowest is not quickened (brought to life), except it die." 1 Corinthians 15:36

As you are reading these verses below, remember that Jesus was raised up only *after* He chose to lay down His life for us in obedience to His and our Father (Jn. 12:23-25, 32; 1 Cor. 15:1-4). God only raises up that which willingly lays itself down and dies. There has to first be a death before there can be a resurrection or raising up.

> "Verily, verily, I say unto you, Except a corn of wheat fall into the ground and die, it abideth alone: but if it die, it bringeth forth much fruit. He that loveth his life shall lose it; and he that hateth his life in this world shall keep it unto life eternal." John 12:24-25

Jesus speaks here of two types of people: **"He that loveth his life"** and **"he that hateth his life in this**

world." What did He say will be the end of each?

"He that loveth his life <u>shall lose it</u>"

> **"he that hateth his life in this world <u>shall keep it</u> unto life eternal"**

Is your life laid down today? Are you crucified with Christ? Have you set your affection on things above and sentenced your self-life to death as you are looking for the soon return of Jesus? (2 Cor. 1:9; Col. 3:1-4; Gal. 2:20; 5:24)

> "He that always waits upon God is ready whensoever He calls ... he is a happy man who so lives as that death at all times may find him at leisure to die." Owen Feltham

As was the case with the Son of God, so it is with us. There has to first be a death before there can be a resurrection or raising up.

> **"The blind receive their sight, and the lame walk, the lepers are cleansed, and the deaf hear, the dead are <u>raised up</u>, and the poor have the gospel preached to them." Matthew 11:5**

> **"And hath <u>raised up</u> an horn of salvation for us in the house of his servant David." Luke 1:69**

> **"Whom God hath <u>raised up</u>, having loosed the pains of death: because it was not possible that he should be holden of it." Acts 2:24**

> **"This Jesus hath God <u>raised up</u>, whereof we all are witnesses." Acts 2:32**

> **"Unto you first God, having <u>raised up</u> his Son Jesus, sent him to bless you, in turning away every one of you from his iniquities." Acts 3:26**

> "The God of our fathers <u>raised up</u> Jesus, whom ye slew and hanged on a tree." Acts 5:30

> "Him God <u>raised up</u> the third day, and shewed him openly." Acts 10:40

Just as God **"raised up"** our LORD Jesus from the dead, He also promised to raise us up as we waive all personal rights to self and count ourselves dead with Christ (Rom. 6:3-5).

> "But if the Spirit of him that raised up Jesus from the dead dwell in you, he that raised up Christ from the dead shall also quicken your mortal bodies by his Spirit that dwelleth in you." Romans 8:11

There is the presence and thread of death, burial, and resurrection woven throughout Scripture. The Gospel is embedded in the Holy Scriptures because death, burial, and resurrection are an integral part of **"the thoughts of his heart,"** which are transmitted and recorded for us in His Word (Ps. 33:11). You may wish to begin watching for the down – up. Here are more words of the LORD which reveal the down-up cadence of the Gospel witnessed throughout Scripture:

> "They that were full have hired out themselves for bread; and they that were hungry ceased: so that the barren hath born seven; and she that hath many children is waxed feeble. <u>The LORD killeth, and maketh alive: he bringeth down to the grave, and bringeth up</u>. The LORD maketh poor, and maketh rich: he bringeth low, and lifteth up. He raiseth up the poor out of the dust, and lifteth up the beggar from the dunghill, to set them among princes, and to make them inherit the throne of glory: for the pillars of the earth are the LORD'S, and he hath set

> the world upon them. He will keep the feet of his saints, and the wicked shall be silent in darkness; for by strength shall no man prevail." 1 Samuel 2:5-9

> "The LORD upholdeth all that fall, and <u>raiseth up</u> all those that be <u>bowed down</u>." Psalms 145:14

> "Persecuted, but not forsaken; cast down, but not destroyed; Always bearing about in the body the dying of the Lord Jesus (death), that the life also of Jesus might be made manifest in our body (resurrection life). For we which <u>live</u> are alway delivered unto <u>death</u> for Jesus' sake, that the <u>life</u> also of Jesus might be made manifest in our mortal flesh. So then <u>death</u> worketh in us, but <u>life</u> in you ... Knowing that he which <u>raised up</u> the Lord Jesus shall <u>raise up</u> us also by Jesus, and shall present us with you." 2 Corinthians 4:9-14

This divine pattern is seen in no more vivid a fashion than in the life and mission of our LORD Jesus:

> "And he began to teach them, that the Son of man must suffer many things, and be rejected of the elders, and of the chief priests, and scribes, and be killed, and after three days rise again." Mark 8:31

The saving Gospel defined:

> "Moreover, brethren, I declare unto you <u>the gospel</u> which I preached unto you, which also ye have received, and wherein ye stand; By which also ye are saved, if ye keep in memory what I preached unto you, unless ye have believed in vain. For I delivered unto you first of

all that which I also received, how that <u>Christ died</u> for our sins according to the scriptures; And that he <u>was buried</u>, and that he <u>rose again</u> the third day according to the scriptures." 1 Corinthians 15:1-4

"Christ died"

"was buried"

"rose again"

Joy Set Forth

Do you work out, or have you ever worked out to train your body for some personal athletic purpose? Why did you work out? Did you work out because it hurt, or because you desired a certain result? Obviously those who work out have a goal to look and/or feel a certain way, right? Yes, people usually work out and endure the burn and pain in order to obtain the desired outcome. Those who exercise or train their bodies are willing to sacrifice and suffer extreme physical discomfort in order to receive the desired results. They long to achieve a certain goal, and that goal is the joy set forth to encourage their endurance and hard work. Once they begin accomplishing their anticipated athletic result, they become glad they started the process, though it induces and requires pain. The desired result is worth the pain.

> **"The desire accomplished is sweet to the soul ..." Proverbs 13:19**

In the same way that the athlete drives himself through daily, painstaking training to accomplish his desired outcome, and is satisfied when that result arrives, so the saint, when he begins to grasp what the Gospel really is as pertains to his daily life, will gladly begin to lay his life downward in order to be raised upward by Christ. In the beginning, when we first hear of and begin pondering the cross and dying to self, perhaps some of us shun the pain. Then, when the Spirit begins leading us to conformity with Christ's death and burial, we take a step forward in obedience, and unfailingly the LORD is there to raise us up in His blessed power. When we begin to experience the Gospel in a personal way – laying down our lives and being *raised up* – *this* writer believes we can acquire a godly addiction to the life and fruit that comes out of this cross and resurrection experience. Paul told us that as he bore in his body the dying of Jesus, the divine life worked in him and through him to bless others (2 Cor. 4:10-12). It is certain that there is more than the dying and burial process – there is the blessed resurrection or raising up. This is one part of what should motivate the disciple to die – that he might see the LORD raise him up in His holy power in this late hour.

Jesus endured His torturous and cruel cross for the joy of redeeming you and me. The pain came before the joy or desired result. There was a desired reaping that made Him willing and obedient to endure the excruciating pain and suffering for our sins (Heb. 12:2).

> **"Looking unto Jesus the author and finisher of our faith; who for the joy that was set before him endured the cross, despising the shame, and is set down at the right hand of the throne of God." Hebrews 12:2**

After Christ endured His cross, the Father raised Him up and gave under His command **"all power in heaven and in earth,"** and gave to **"him a name which is above every name."** (Matt. 28:18-20)

> **"Look not every man on his own things, but every man also on the things of others. Let this mind be in you, which was also in Christ**

> **Jesus: Who, being in the form of God, thought it not robbery to be equal with God: But made himself of no reputation, and took upon him the form of a servant, and was made in the likeness of men: And being found in fashion as a man, he humbled himself, and became obedient unto death, even the death of the cross. Wherefore God also hath highly exalted him, and given him a name which is above every name: That at the name of Jesus every knee should bow, of things in heaven, and things in earth, and things under the earth; And that every tongue should confess that Jesus Christ is Lord, to the glory of God the Father. Wherefore, my beloved, as ye have always obeyed, not as in my presence only, but now much more in my absence, work out your own salvation with fear and trembling. For it is God which worketh in you both to will and to do of his good pleasure." Philippians 2:4-13**

If Jesus came to the earth, divesting Himself into the form of a man, humbling Himself from Godhood to servant, how much more shall we humble ourselves, laying down our lives for Christ and His beloved people, and precious souls who need His salvation? Is our descent not a far lesser trip than was His? It should be a short journey, right – in comparison to His? As the Most High God and Creator of all that is, Christ's condescension to the lowly place of mere humankind was a distant journey (though He was the sinless Son of man).

In this magnificent passage (Philippians 2), we just read of God becoming a man. Not only did He who made all that is, come to this sin-cursed earth incarnated into humanity, the Eternal Word came as a Servant to humble Himself and become **"obedient unto death, even the death of the cross."** God the Father therefore **"hath**

highly exalted him, and given him a name which is above every name." Jesus promised to give all of His saints who overcome, a **"new name."** Read these two verses from Revelation closely, okay:

> **"He that hath an ear, let him hear what the Spirit saith unto the churches; To him that overcometh will I give to eat of the hidden manna, and will give him a white stone, and in the stone a new name written, which no man knoweth saving he that receiveth it." Revelation 2:17**
>
> **"Him that overcometh will I make a pillar in the temple of my God, and he shall go no more out: and I will write upon him the name of my God, and the name of the city of my God, which is new Jerusalem, which cometh down out of heaven from my God: and I will write upon him my new name." Revelation 3:12**

Christ tells us here that a brand **"new name"** and a permanent place as a **"pillar in the temple of my God"** awaits all who answer His call to repent and be saved, and who also overcome the flesh, the world, and the devil. These are the remnant who will be *raised up* to reign with Christ eternally – **"they ... are ... called, and chosen, and faithful."** Jesus said that those who overcome and will be raised up to reign with Him eternally are not only **"called"** by God, but also **"chosen, and faithful."** There is a partnership and agreement. God sovereignly calls them and chooses them and they choose to be **"faithful,"** enduring to the end, loving not their lives even unto death (Rev. 12:11; 17:14). The honest student of Scripture refuses to acquiesce to the diabolical myth that supposes that man has no part in the reception and retention of salvation. See the book, *Lie of the Ages*, at www.SafeGuardYourSoul.com.

> **"These shall make war with the Lamb, and the Lamb shall overcome them: for he is Lord of lords, and King of kings: and they that are with him are called, and chosen, and faithful." Revelation 17:14**

As our LORD came and was obedient to His Father in all things, how shall we, who are purchased by His precious blood, not become obedient unto the death of the self-life, setting aside our own will and agenda, waiving all personal rights, and girding ourselves to become His servants? Will He who raised Christ up to the highest place in the Universe not lift us up to please and glorify Him here and now, and to reign with Him eternally?

> **"Blessed and holy is he that hath part in the first resurrection: on such the second death hath no power, but they shall be priests of God and of Christ, and shall reign with him a thousand years." Revelation 20:6**

Beloved, God is working in each of His saints **"both to will and to do of his good pleasure."** (Phil. 2:13) **"His good pleasure"** is to get us to become **"obedient unto death, even the death of the cross"** so that He can raise us up in His holy power to be Christ-like, and to rule with Him in the coming world. This is the mind of Christ (Phil. 2:5-13).

PRAYER: *Holy Father, please grant my heart to see beyond this life and into the much larger scope of the coming world, where Christ will reign supreme and the government shall rest upon His shoulders alone. Anoint me with Your Holy Ghost to the burial of my sinful self-life. I love You, Jesus, and thank You for Your perfect sacrifice for me. Father, I know and believe that You will raise me up here and eternally if I will trust You and obey Your command for me to become obedient unto the death of my self-life. I here and now joyfully and willingly submit my life* *to Your lordship. Into Your hands I now commend my spirit. Amen.*

Capture Points

- Who did the LORD promise to raise up? 2 Corinthians 4:10-14.

- What should every believer bear in his body daily? 2 Corinthians 4:10-11.

- What works in and through Christ's saints, as death to self works in them? 2 Corinthians 4:12.

SafeGuardYourSoul.com

Chapter Five

The Laid Down Life
Living in the Spirit

> **"And they that are Christ's have crucified the flesh with the affections and lusts. If we live in the Spirit, let us also walk in the Spirit." Galatians 5:24-25**

Living in the Spirit and not in the flesh is a settled issue with the remnant. They **"have crucified the flesh"** and the evil the sinful nature would do. It's a done deal - they **"HAVE crucified the flesh"** that Christ the LORD might reign in their mortal bodies.

> **"Likewise reckon (count) ye also yourselves to be dead indeed unto sin, but alive unto God through Jesus Christ our Lord. Let not sin**

> therefore reign in your mortal body, that ye should obey it in the lusts thereof. Neither yield ye your members *as* instruments of unrighteousness unto sin: but yield yourselves unto God, as those that are alive from the dead, and your members as instruments of righteousness unto God. For sin shall not have dominion over you (because you have accounted yourself dead): for ye are not under the law, but under grace. What then? shall we sin, because we are not under the law, but under grace? God forbid. Know ye not, that to whom ye yield yourselves servants to obey, his servants ye are to whom ye obey; whether of sin unto death, or of obedience unto righteousness? But God be thanked, that ye were the servants of sin, but ye have obeyed from the heart that form of doctrine which was delivered you. Being then made free from sin, ye became the servants of righteousness." Romans 6:11-18

The **"form of doctrine"** delivered by Christ and His holy apostles in the original Gospel, included the accounting of one's life now dead and then being raised up by Christ, with His life-giving grace operating within to please Him fully (see also Rom. 12:1-3; 1 Cor. 15:10; 2 Cor. 12:9).

God's desire, plan, and command is that His people reign victoriously in this life over sin and the enemy.

> **"For if by one man's offence death reigned by one; much more they which receive abundance of grace and of the gift of righteousness shall reign in life by one, Jesus Christ." Romans 5:17**

Let's peer again into the words of our LORD found in John 12:

> **"And Jesus answered them, saying, The hour is come, that the Son of man should be glorified. Verily, verily, I say unto you, Except a corn of wheat fall into the ground and die, it abideth alone: but if it die, it bringeth forth much fruit. He that loveth his life shall lose it; and he that hateth his life in this world shall keep it unto life eternal. If any man serve me, let him follow me; and where I am, there shall also my servant be: if any man serve me, him will my Father honour." John 12:23-26**

Laying down our lives is paramount to walking with Jesus. It is His command (Lk. 9:23-24; 14:33, etc.). He raises up in new life those that are **"bowed down"** before Him (Ps. 145:14). The seed (**"corn"**) is planted or buried alive, and is resurrected by God to a life of glory and blessing and grace to endure and be brought through all chastening, difficulties, persecutions, circumstances, trials, and testings. *Without a death, there can be no resurrection.* This death to the self-life is volitional and ongoing in this life – **"I die daily."** (1 Cor. 15:31)

> **"He must increase, but I *must* decrease." John 3:30**

As we are blessed to be **"planted together in the likeness of his death,"** so **"we shall be also in the likeness of his resurrection."**

> **"Know ye not, that so many of us as were baptized into Jesus Christ were baptized into his death? Therefore we are buried with him by baptism into death: that like as Christ was raised up from the dead by the glory of the Father, even so we also should walk in newness of**

life. For if we have been planted together in the likeness of his death, we shall be also *in the likeness* of his resurrection." Romans 6:3-5**

This is rightfully the most popular Bible passage on water baptism, and explains what the meaning and purpose of water baptism is. At water baptism, we are buried in water, figuratively dying to the old man, the man of sin, and resurrected by the risen Savior and LORD to a new life in which He reigns supreme.

"And if Christ *be* in you, the body is dead because of sin; but the Spirit *is* life because of righteousness. But if the Spirit of him that raised up Jesus from the dead dwell in you, he that raised up Christ from the dead shall also quicken your mortal bodies by his Spirit that dwelleth in you." Romans 8:10-11

There are symptoms in the life of one who is not buried. The disciple who is buried with Christ is **"dead to sin."** (Rom. 6:2) When we argue to justify the things we do in this life and call those who point them out "legalistic," it is symptomatic of a life that is not laid down. When we argue against the truth (the Bible says **"Lie not against the truth"** in James 3:14) when we are shown it, we manifest the rebellion in our hearts because our lives are not authentically laid out before the LORD. The **"corn of wheat"** must be planted and remain planted in order to bud and bring forth new life. The one whose life is laid down does not make excuses when he realizes that he has sin. No, instead he rejoices to be yet more delivered and in the place of blessing and holiness with the One He delights to please and serve.

Aren't we the temple of the Holy Ghost and commanded to **"cleanse ourselves from all filthiness of the flesh and spirit, perfecting holiness in the fear of God"?** (2 Cor. 7:1)

If we still have habitual sin in our lives, we should know that we are not buried with Christ. If we were, His life would be teeming in us and causing us to put away sinfulness. Overcoming sin happens when we bury the old man of sin by nailing it to the cross. God is with us to do such (Rom. 8:13; Phil. 2:12-13).

> **"For even hereunto were ye called: because Christ also suffered for us, leaving us an example, that ye should follow his steps: Who did no sin, neither was guile found in his mouth: Who, when he was reviled, reviled not again; when he suffered, he threatened not; but committed *himself* to him that judgeth righteously: Who his own self bare our sins in his own body on the tree, that we, being dead to sins, should live unto righteousness: by whose stripes ye were healed." 1 Peter 2:21-24**

The LORD looks upon the hearts of men (1 Sam. 16:7). Getting our hearts right with God begins with laying down the right to ourselves and releasing ourselves into the unfailing hands of the One who made us and gives us the breath of life (Lk. 23:46). This is in following the ultimate example of our LORD Jesus, who came and laid down His sinless life for us (1 Pet. 2:21; 4:1).

Let's check our deadness. Let's see how dead we are to this world system and all of its arrogant rebellion against the God of the universe and all that is: Do we defend our "right" to fill our minds and hearts with the evil things that are blatantly and subtly portrayed on some TV and radio programming (and other forms of modern media)? If so, the fleshly nature is not dead but is still alive, and we are therefore not raised to new life.

Perhaps it is true (as has been stated by some) that a person can be known by what he laughs at or finds humorous. What do we laugh at? What do we find entertaining? **"Charity ... Rejoiceth not in iniquity, but rejoiceth in the truth."** (1 Cor. 13:4, 6)

Laying down our lives requires a deliberate, willful decision. Believers are called to be circumspect (fully orbed in holiness) and are not to glorify anything the LORD calls profane (Prov. 17:15; 24:24; Isa. 5:20-24; Ezek. 44:23; Eph. 5:15-17).

Why crucify the flesh when there is no reason to do such? When a new believer is told that he is "eternally secure" or *once saved always saved,* why then should he get sanctified, live a repentant life, be wholly set apart to the LORD, be matured and equipped to do ministry, or prepare for the soon return of Jesus Christ?

The following brief and yet convicting commentary is taken from the *Life in the Spirit Study Bible* concerning Romans 1:32. First let's view the Biblical text, then the commentary.

> **"Who knowing the judgment of God, that they which commit such things are worthy of death, not only do the same, but have pleasure in them that do them." Romans 1:32**

> **"'HAVE PLEASURE IN THEM THAT DO THEM'.** Paul's last word on general human sinfulness is God's condemnation of a condition even more damning than the practice, i.e. supporting, approving, and encouraging evil by taking pleasure in the immoral actions of others. This disposition is the ultimate in depravity - vicarious enjoyment of lust and evil. Sin becomes entertainment. (1) The word 'have pleasure' (Gk. suneudokeo) means 'are pleased with,' 'delight in,' or 'give approval to,' and points to the casual enjoyment of the sins of others that prevails in human society. (2) Today we know that great harm is produced by the portrayal

of immorality that dominates the entertainment media; yet many consent to it and derive pleasure from it. Being entertained by watching other people sin and engage in ungodly actions, even while you yourself abstain, brings you under the same condemnation of God as those engaging in such evil practices. Iniquity is intensified in any society where sin meets with no inhibition from the disapproval of others and where people enjoy watching it. (3) Hence, those (and especially those who profess faith in Christ) who use the immoral actions of others for entertainment and enjoyment, are directly contributing to public opinion favorable to immorality and, therefore, to the corruption and eternal damnation of an indefinite number of other people. This sin is worthy of death and will be exposed and judged at the final day of judgment (2 Thess. 2:12)." p. 1729

Concerning the many things in this sinful world that would draw our affections away from Jesus Christ and blur that pure-focused disposition, the Psalmist wrote:

"I will set no wicked thing before mine eyes: I hate the work of them that turn aside; it shall not cleave to me." Psalms 101:3

Do we seek to protect our "right" to continue relishing the things of this world, which are despised of God? See 1 John 2:14-17. The Bible tells us that those who love this world system and the things in it hate God and are His enemies – regardless of what they profess (Tit. 1:16; James 4:4).

When we live out the Word, He promised persecution would come, and instructed us to rejoice (Matt. 5:10-12; Mk. 4:17; 1 Pet. 4:12). Have you ever been persecuted by other "believers" and called legalistic because you chose not to watch a movie that mocks at what God calls sin? I guess I have seen people do this to truth-speakers for so long, that it has little affect anymore, other than inducing a concern for where they really are in their hearts. Seeking to be upright in one's ways is not legalistic – it is biblical. The Word instructs us to **"walk circumspectly,"** which means fully obedient – exactly, diligently, and perfectly.

> **"See then that ye walk circumspectly, not as fools, but as wise, Redeeming the time, because the days are evil. Wherefore be ye not unwise, but understanding what the will of the Lord *is*. And be not drunk with wine, wherein is excess; but be filled with the Spirit; Speaking to yourselves in psalms and hymns and spiritual songs, singing and making melody in your heart to the Lord; Giving thanks always for all things unto God and the Father in the name of our Lord Jesus Christ." Ephesians 5:15-20**

> **"And in all things that I have said unto you be circumspect: and make no mention of the name of other gods, neither let it be heard out of thy mouth." Exodus 23:13**

What the LORD tells us in Proverbs 26:4-5, is that when we join a fool in his folly (foolishness), we become as guilty as he is and perpetuate this sinfulness in his life, and more importantly – we offend the holiness of the LORD we claim to be serving.

What we partake of and/or laugh at reveals who we really are. If all these sinful things and justification of them are still alive in us, we do not have a laid down life.

Apparently, according to the Word of God, returning laughter when we witness foolishness (folly) confirms the person we are laughing at in his folly and causes us to partake of his foolishness and deeds.

> **"Fools make a mock at sin: but among the righteous** *there is* **favour." Proverbs 14:9**

> **"Folly (foolishness)** *is joy to him that is* **destitute of wisdom: but a man of understanding walketh uprightly." Proverbs 15:21**

Yes, laughter is a blessing and there is a **"time to laugh"** and to rejoice, yet we are not made free from sin by the blood of Christ to laugh at evil things (Eccl. 3:4). *LORD, please bless us to be purified in our hearts and to rejoice and laugh more – for the right reasons! Please grant us Your joy, Jesus! Amen.*

> **"A merry heart doeth good** *like* **a medicine: but a broken spirit drieth the bones." Proverbs 17:22**

The fear of the LORD is the beginning of wisdom and knowledge, and those who have it walk uprightly - they walk biblically in the Holy Spirit of grace and not legalistically. They have joy from Jesus and are the most blessed people in the world.

> **"The LORD upholdeth all that fall, and <u>raiseth up</u> all** *those that be* **bowed down." Psalms 145:14**

Here we see once again that the LORD limits His resurrection power to those who choose to **"be bowed down"** in humility before Him.

Beloved, our LORD is calling us to lay down our lives like Christ did – that He might fully possess us. Bow down before His holiness that He may raise you up His way. Let it all go. Die to justifying your sins. Before this day expires, get alone with the Savior and release the life He gave to you back to Him. Completely relinquish control as you cry out like Jesus did on the cross when dying for us - **"Father, into thy hands I commend my spirit."** (Lk. 23:46) Give up the ghost. Cease living life on your terms. Lay your whole life at His feet, and let Him raise you up in newness of life in the Holy Spirit and reign supreme in your body.

The Path of Our LORD Jesus

> "Although Jesus was rich in all the divine fullness of His divine nature, He become poor and emptied Himself (see 2 Cor. 8:9). In other words, He determined not to speak His own words, follow His own scheme and plan, or work His mighty works in His own might. Rather, He became the channel and instrument through which His Father spoke, worked, and reconciled the world unto Himself. Let us, like Jesus, empty ourselves that we might be filled with God's mercy, power, and love." F.B. Meyer, *The Best of F.B. Meyer,* p. 180

Jesus was to be glorified by the Father in laying down His life for all men (Jn. 15:13).

> **"... nevertheless not my will, but thine, be done..." Luke 22:42**

He laid down His own will because of the immeasurable love He has for each of us.

> **"Greater love hath no man than this, that a man lay down his life for his friends." John 15:13**

Do we love Jesus Christ in return? How much do I love Him? Will I lay down my whole existence before Him, knowing He will raise me up to new life and fruitfulness as He lives His life through me? Is this not the essence of Galatians 2:20?

> "I am crucified with Christ: nevertheless I live; yet not I, but Christ liveth in me: and the life which I now live in the flesh I live by the faith of the Son of God, who loved me, and gave himself for me." **Galatians 2:20**

He must increase and we must decrease, that He might be glorified in us, and we might be the living epistles He has called us to be. When Jesus is reigning in a person's life, it is obvious. His holy and impelling presence is the life that exudes from that person instead of the stench of the self-centered and selfish nature (Jn. 3:30). At this place of resurrection life, the LORD who made and redeemed us is greatly glorified and pleased, and His fruit is being yielded.

> "Be ye therefore followers of God, as dear children; And walk in love, as Christ also hath loved us, and hath given himself for us an offering and a sacrifice to God for a sweetsmelling savour." **Ephesians 5:1-2**

Finding that place with God in prayer is where the laid down life begins. May I suggest that you begin with prayerfully, and from deep within, citing Galatians 2:20 aloud?

> "Deep calleth unto deep at the noise of thy waterspouts: all thy waves and thy billows are gone over me." **Psalms 42:7**

PRAYER: *Please draw me deeper in You, LORD Jesus. Father in Heaven, You sent Your only begotten Son to die for me in order that I might be raised up in new life, both in this brief life and eternally. I love You, Jesus, and ask You to lead me to that crucified life that You lived when here on earth. Quicken me by Your Holy Spirit and fill me afresh, O LORD, that this life You gave might be fully fruitful and pleasing to Thee. Lord, I am watching and praying* *in light of Your soon return. Amen.*

Capture Points

- What is an earmark characteristic of all those who are truly and presently serving Christ? Galatians 5:24

- *Prayerfully and with deep meditation, write out Galatians 5:24 on an index card (KJV recommended).*

- According to Psalms 145:14, who does God limit His resurrection power to?

Chapter Six

"Walk While Ye Have the Light, Lest Darkness Come Upon You"
John 12:35

> "Walk while ye have the light, lest darkness come upon you: for he that walketh in darkness knoweth not whither he goeth." John 12:35

Not one of us is exempt from coming under **"the power of darkness."** (Lk. 22:53) During this **"hour"** of **"the power of darkness,"** even the apostle Peter **"followed afar off"** due to His momentarily shunning of the light of Christ in his personal life (Lk. 22:54). He was prayerless. The Scripture also tells us here that in his state of spiritual darkness, **"Peter sat down among them."** (Lk. 22:55) This means that instead of coming out from among them and being sanctified, Peter began to assimilate with and become like the world's people (1 Cor. 15:33; 2 Cor. 6:14-18). This disciple of Jesus had neglected communion and fellowship in prayer with the Father, and was therefore not full of Christ's light and power to resist darkness and depravity of soul. He was therefore being absorbed by the world. Ever been there yourself?

> "Pray often; for prayer is a shield to the soul, a sacrifice to God, and a scourge for Satan." John Bunyan

Satan, who desired to sift Peter, was overcome due to the intercession of Christ (Lk. 22:31-32). Peter had neglected his relationship or communion with Jesus (Lk. 22:54). **"The power of darkness"** caused the apostle Peter to slide back and follow Christ **"afar off."**

> **"Watch and pray, that ye enter not into temptation: the spirit indeed is willing, but the flesh is weak." Matthew 26:41**

If God were going to do it all for us, why did He command us to **"watch and pray"**?

The only hope we have to subdue the dictates of the sinful nature is to be filled to overflowing with the presence of God, which renders powerless the sinful nature that dwells in us (Matt. 26:41; Rom. 8:13-14; 1 Cor. 9:27). In order to see this subduing come to pass, the believer must obey Christ's command to **"watch and pray."** If he doesn't, he will assuredly **"enter into temptation"** and fall.

Consider what we read in Mark's account of Peter's denial of Christ and what led to such a backslidden state:

> **"And he cometh, and findeth them sleeping, and saith unto Peter, Simon, sleepest thou?**

> **couldest not thou watch one hour? Watch ye and pray, lest ye enter into temptation. The spirit truly *is* ready, but the flesh *is* weak. And again he went away, and prayed, and spake the same words. And when he returned, he found them asleep again, (for their eyes were heavy,) neither wist (knew) they what to answer him." Mark 14:37-40**

Peter slept instead of communing with the heavenly Father in prayer. Have we done likewise? Are we doing so now?

May God bless each of us to cast off slothfulness and be engaged with Him in the innermost parts of our hearts and the daily activities of praise and prayer that facilitate such blessed communion. May our affections be set upon Him who is worthy to be praised (Col. 3:1-4).

> **"Slothfulness casteth into a deep sleep; and an idle soul shall suffer hunger. He that keepeth the commandment keepeth his own soul;** *but* **he that despiseth his ways shall die." Proverbs 19:15-16**

According to this above Bible passage, where does **"slothfulness"** cast (throw) us? – **"into a deep sleep (spiritually)."** Also, what will be suffered by the **"idle (prayerless) soul"**? – spiritual **"hunger."**

> "People do not drift toward holiness. Apart from grace-driven effort, people do not gravitate toward godliness, prayer, obedience to Scripture, faith and delight in the Lord. We drift toward disobedience and call it freedom; we drift toward prayerlessness and delude ourselves into thinking we have escaped legalism; we slide toward godlessness and convince ourselves we have been liberated." D.A. Carson, *For the Love of God*, vol. 2

The daily cross must have its place in my life. Christ must take center stage. I must deny the self-life by presenting my body and its evil inclinations as a living sacrifice to God, which is my reasonable service (Rom. 12:1). For the love and preeminence of Jesus, the cross – the implement of death to self – must be central to my life that I might live by and in the power of His resurrection life (2 Cor. 4:10-11). There is no more important place that this cross must be applied than in the life of prayer – daily. Prayerlessness must be attacked head on with a deliberate scheduling of God first in my personal life. Prayerlessness must be a sin of the past, crucified and superseded by a life of daily and intimate communion with my LORD and Savior.

The life of perpetual prayer is the manifestation of a moment-to-moment submitting of oneself to God as a living sacrifice, buried deep in the soil of Christ's death. The divine reciprocation is the raising upward of that bowed down believer on the wings of His grace and power (Isa. 37:31; Rom. 6:3-5; 8:11; 12:1). This is when we begin to experience truly knowing Him and the power of His resurrection, and the fellowship of His sufferings through persecution (Phil. 3:10).

> "I need to experience fellowship with Christ on His cross if the Spirit is really to take possession of me." Andrew Murray, *199 Treasures of Wisdom on Talking with God*, no. 85

Beloved, prayerlessness is all it takes to fall away from Christ. A myriad of Scriptures testify to this truth. Here's one passage for example:

> **"And he cometh unto the disciples, and findeth them asleep, and saith unto Peter, What, could ye not watch with me one hour? Watch and pray, that ye enter not into temptation: the spirit indeed *is* willing, but the flesh *is* weak."**

Matthew 26:40-41

By Christ's words here we know that all those who don't **"watch and pray"** will of certainty **"enter ... into temptation."**

> "Prayer warfare simply means holding unceasingly to the power of the finished work of Christ." Matthew Washington

Neglecting daily fellowship with Jesus is turning from the light and toward darkness. Prayerlessness is an intentional decision. Such a deliberate choice carries grave consequences and jeopardy of soul. The life of prayer must displace such a life of neglecting the One who **"washed us from our sins in his own blood"** and is to be our **"first love."** (Rev. 1:5; 2:4-5) Shunning the light of Christ through neglecting communion with Him, will without fail lead to darkness of heart. Consider the following verses:

> **"Give glory to the LORD your God, before he cause darkness, and before your feet stumble upon the dark mountains, and, while ye look for light, he turn it into the shadow of death, *and* make *it* gross darkness." Jeremiah 13:16**

> **"Walk while ye have the light, lest darkness come upon you: for he that walketh in darkness knoweth not whither he goeth." John 12:35**

The threat and **"power of darkness"** looms over each saint of Christ as it did with Peter. All it takes to come under **"the power of darkness"** is to cease to **"give glory to the LORD."** In order to experience **"fellowship one with another,"** the disciple must not neglect walking **"in the light as he is in the light."** (Jer. 13:16; Jn. 12:35; 1 Jn. 1:7)

> "...our fellowship *is* with the Father, and with his Son Jesus Christ ... If we say that we have fellowship with him, and walk in darkness, we lie, and do not the truth: But if we walk in the light, as he is in the light, we have fellowship one with another, and the blood of Jesus Christ his Son cleanseth us from all sin." 1 John 1:3, 6-7

In this important passage in 1 John 1, we see that His light in and upon our understanding is directly connected with our relationship or **"fellowship"** with **"the Father, and with his Son Jesus Christ."** The ongoing blessing of **"fellowship"** with Him is contingent upon the **"if"** of our **"walk in the light, as he is in the light."**

We bask in His divine light as we commune in His holy and precious presence, walking in obedience to His Word. In His light we see light, and it shines into the darkness of our souls, exposing the things He wishes to remove (Ps. 36:9; Prov. 20:27).

"Darkness" has **"power,"** otherwise the Holy Spirit would not have inspired the words, **"the power of darkness."** (Lk. 22:53) Darkness will darken the light in us if diligent effort and conformity is not enacted by the recipient of the salvation of Christ. The desire to know Him and the power of His resurrection and fellowship of His sufferings will compel the seeking saint to abide in close fellowship with Christ (Ps. 27:4; Prov. 18:1; Matt. 6:22-23; Phil. 3:10).

In the Garden of Gethsemane, Jesus had just submitted Himself to the Father for the crucifixion He was getting ready to suffer for the sins of the whole world. In His agony and the further surrender of His own individual will, He cried, **"not my will but thine, be done."** (Lk. 22:42) **"The power of darkness"** had no power over Christ because He was submitted to His Father. The same is true for us.

> **"Submit yourselves therefore to God. Resist the devil, and he will flee from you." James 4:7**

The prince of darkness is given no place in the lives of those who are submitted to God. They are able to resist him and his schemes, which they are able to see by the light of Christ in them (Ps. 36:9; 2 Cor. 2:11; 1 Jn. 1:7). Here's the divine prescription:

"Submit yourselves therefore to God"

"Resist (set yourself against) the devil"

"and he will flee from you"

The darkness of the dark one, and that which is associated and given to those who are not obedient, can have no reign over the children of God – those truly submitted to the LORD.

Darkness can only possess those who are not with Jesus – because all who are not **"with"** Jesus are definitively **"against"** Him (Matt. 12:30). All who do not choose to be **"with"** Christ, the Person, in obedience and in His mission, will come under the dark shadow of **"the power of darkness"** just as Peter, the Jews, and the civil rulers did.

Like Peter the apostle, believers are not exempt from being in darkness. Sin causes the hardening of the heart and darkness in the life of any person who does not obey the light of truth.

In our daily walk, all darkness is expelled by Him who is **"the light"** when **"we walk in the light as he is in the light."** (Jn. 8:12; 1 Jn. 1:7)

Any day in which I am not denying myself and taking up

my cross, I am choosing to love self more than Christ, not following Jesus, and living according to the sinful nature. Can you relate? On the days in which I am choosing to respond to the love God showed forth in His **"only begotten Son,"** I am consumed with the fellowship of His Spirit and granted divine grace and power to please Him with abundant fruitfulness in all things (Jn. 3:16; 15:16).

Those who choose not to daily schedule God first (with the highest priority, first place), will inevitably be hurled into spiritual darkness. **"Slothfulness"** in fellowshipping with the One who bled for our sins, will certainly throw us into spiritual darkness (Prov. 19:15). Peter experienced such; he slept while he should have been praying diligently, and as a result he denied Christ thrice (Mk. 14:38-72; Lk. 22:45-46). Those who choose to engage their hearts and lives in a life of prayer communion with Christ, will walk in His holy light which dispels darkness from their hearts and prevents the horrible condition of a darkened heart. Those who do not obey the Word are **"deceiving"** their own selves and becoming darkened in heart, calloused, and hardened through the deceitfulness of sin (Ps. 119:130; Prov. 14:14; Jer. 30:21; Joel 2:13; Heb. 3:12-15; James 1:22; 1 Jn. 1:3-9).

Every single person who is not busy about the heavenly **"Father's business,"** is not following Christ but rather serving self, and **"no man can serve two maters."** (Matt. 6:24; Lk. 2:49) According to Jesus, that person is not **"with"** Him but rather **"against"** Him and scattering people abroad instead of gathering them to Him (Matt. 12:30). He that is not actively doing God's will/Word is fruitless and separated from God – **"EVERY tree that bringeth not forth good fruit is hewn down, and cast into the fire."** (Matt. 7:19) God saved us by His grace to be His very **"workmanship"** who say to the lost, **"Come."** (Eph. 2:8-10; Rev. 22:17) Those who are not literally doing God's will are liars and the truth is not in them – they are utterly deceived (James 1:22; 1 Jn. 2:4).

There are tens of thousands of false leaders in the church world today. They lead their audiences to self-indulgence instead of self-denial. They never deal with the words of the One they claim to serve when He told us that any person who would follow Him must **"deny himself, and take up his cross, and follow"** Him (Matt. 16:24). Any person who does otherwise is not truly following Christ who is the only way to God and Heaven, and is therefore not going there (Jn. 14:6).

We are bought by the blood of Christ and made new creatures in Him, and we must ask ourselves what His Word says concerning His will and mission for us, lest we be misled by the **"many false prophets"** He repeatedly foretold would seek to lead us away from Him (Matt. 7:15; 24:3-5, 11, 24; Lk. 6:39; 1 Jn. 4:1). Jesus told us that we would know **"false prophets … by their fruits."** (Matt. 7:16-20) **"Their fruits"** concern their doctrine and whether they are leading according to the Word of God, or misleading by not simply declaring the pure Word (Isa. 8:20; Ezek. 3:4; 2 Tim. 4:2-5; 1 Pet. 4:11). Under the direct inspiration of the Holy Spirit, a known true prophet, the apostle Paul, wrote these following words concerning reconciled saints:

> **"Therefore if any man be in Christ, he is a new creature: old things are passed away; behold, all things are become new. And all things are of God, who hath reconciled us to himself by Jesus Christ, and <u>hath given to us the ministry of reconciliation</u>; To wit, that God was in Christ, reconciling the world unto himself, not imputing their trespasses unto them; and hath committed unto us the word of reconciliation. Now then we are ambassadors for Christ, as though God did beseech you by us: we pray you in**

> **Christ's stead, be ye reconciled to God. For he hath made him to be sin for us, who knew no sin; that we might be made the righteousness of God in him." 2 Corinthians 5:17-21**

Jesus was made sin for us and has found and reconciled us to Himself and the Father via His blood. He **"hath given to us the ministry of reconciliation."** Got any questions for Him about this? Pretty simple call and instruction, isn't it?

God gives those He saves the command to **"go ye into all the world"** and to **"preach the gospel to every creature,"** and to teach all men all the things He has and is teaching us (Matt. 28:18-20; Mk. 16:15). We who are genuinely His, are not our own but bought with the price of His very blood. Having been made new creatures in Christ, we have been given **"the ministry of reconciliation,"** and not the ministry of prosperity, seeking purpose, enjoying our best life now, or any other self-serving, utterly rebellious and sin-filled agenda (1 Cor. 6:19-20; 2 Cor. 5:17-21; 2 Tim. 3:1-7, 13). If one is truly saved – **"reconciled to God"** – he is seeking to see other precious souls saved. Any person who claims to be a follower of Jesus and does not seek to save that which was lost, is utterly deluded (Mk. 4:19; Lk. 19:10). This was Jesus' mission and it's the mission of all who know Him. **"Many"** will be shocked on Judgment Day (Matt. 7:21-23).

Jesus told us that if we are following Him, we are becoming soul winners.

> **"And Jesus said unto them, Come ye after me, and I will make you to become fishers of men." Mark 1:17**

Jesus Christ shed His precious blood to redeem us, and then sent those who are His to go tell others of His sacrifice, and redeeming love, which is the only way they can be rescued from sure damnation (Mk. 9:42-49; 16:15-16). He gave to us the ministry, word, and work of reconciliation – not prosperity or obtaining things for ourselves in this life. Such pursuit is clear evidence of an apostate heart which, if not repented of, will result in eternal damnation (1 Tim. 4:1-3; 2 Pet. 2:1-4).

"Christ Jesus came into the world to save sinners," and those He saves become useful and fruitful vessels of His, winning other lost souls to Him (1 Tim. 1:15). His true remnant disciples are not self-seeking but rather seek to please Him who bought them back from a life of sin, separation, and certain damnation.

Being **"ambassadors for Christ"** involves winning souls for whom He came and bled, and not procuring things to ourselves (2 Cor. 5:17-21). Those who aren't about the **"Father's business,"** are about their own business and have become spiritual adulterers who have left Christ as their **"first love,"** having procured to themselves a false god (Exod. 20:3; Ezek. 14:3; Lk. 2:49; Eph. 5:5-7; 1 Jn. 5:21; Rev. 21:8; 22:15). **"Ye adulterers and adulteresses, know ye not that the friendship of the world is enmity with God? whosoever therefore will be a friend of the world is the enemy of God."** (James 4:4)

Any leader who is not involving, exhorting, and helping those he oversees to win lost souls – to see them reconciled to the LORD – is a false prophet. Run for your life – he is not teaching according to or fulfilling Christ's clearly stated kingdom purpose which is **"to seek and to save that which was lost."** (Lk. 19:10; Eph. 4:11-12).

If a person truly knows the One that came and bled on a wooden cross for the sins of the whole world, that person will be concerned and active about winning lost souls to Him. Jesus Christ told us definitively that His true Bride says to the lost, **"Come."** (Rev. 22:17) Those who have the **"witness"** in themselves of being born of God, call others to repent and be saved (Rom. 8:16; 1 Jn. 5:8-10). There are a plethora of excuses people make to justify their blatant disobedience to the command of the Savior to **"Go ye into all the world and preach the gospel to every creature,"** but none of them are valid – not one (Mk. 16:15). Aren't you glad Christ didn't make excuses for not coming to die for your sins? Many who claim to know Jesus want to say that evangelism just isn't *their* "gift," or that they don't have enough knowledge, etc., but no excuse for disobeying the LORD is legitimate. There are several groupings of gifts in the New Testament Scriptures, and evangelism is *not* listed in one of those lists of gifts – because evangelism is not a gift, but rather a command of the LORD Jesus Christ – to **"Go."** So, are our lives laid down in such a way that we are living out what He commanded us? Listen to the LORD's voice here in 2 Corinthians 5:19:

> **"To wit, that God was in Christ, reconciling the world unto himself, not imputing their trespasses unto them; and hath committed unto us the word of reconciliation." 2 Corinthians 5:19**

Those who authentically know the LORD are presently using their time, talents, and treasures to reach precious lost souls for whom Jesus bled (Matt. 26:28; 1 Tim. 1:15). Any person who is not obeying the LORD clearly reveals that he is not truly submitted to the LORD, but is rather serving himself – a false god that cannot save his eternal soul from everlasting damnation (Exod. 20:3; Isa. 64:6; James 4:6-10).

Jesus is the "Light of the World"

> **"In him was life; and the life was the light of men. And the light shineth in darkness; and the darkness comprehended it not. There was a man sent from God, whose name *was* John.**

> **The same came for a witness, to bear witness of the Light, that all *men* through him might believe. He was not that Light, but *was sent* to bear witness of that Light. *That* was the true Light, which lighteth every man that cometh into the world. He was in the world, and the world was made by him, and the world knew him not. He came unto his own, and his own received him not. But as many as received him, to them gave he power to become the sons of God, *even* to them that believe on his name: Which were born, not of blood, nor of the will of the flesh, nor of the will of man, but of God." John 1:4-13**

Jesus tells us in Matthew 6 that if the focus of our lives is clear and single in purpose, pointed straight on to Him, that our whole body shall be filled with the light of Him who is **"the light of the world."** (Jn. 8:12) Conversely, if our eye or focus be not on Jesus, our whole body shall be filled with darkness.

> **"The light of the body is the eye: if therefore thine eye be single, thy whole body shall be full of light. But if thine eye be evil, thy whole body shall be full of darkness. If therefore the light that is in thee be darkness, how great *is* that darkness!" Matthew 6:22-23**

Since God's **"light is come into the world"** through Christ's coming, men who shun, neglect, or turn from it will suffer **"condemnation."** Those who **"cometh to the light"** will be blessed to have their evil **"deeds ... reproved,"** or surfaced and solved by the Savior.

> **"And this is the condemnation, that light is come into the world, and men loved darkness rather than light, because their deeds were evil. For every one that doeth evil hateth the light,**

neither cometh to the light, lest his deeds should be reproved. But he that doeth truth cometh to the light, that his deeds may be made manifest, that they are wrought in God." John 3:19-21

Of Christ, the **"light of the world,"** the Scripture says:

> "In him was life; and the life was the light of men. And the light shineth in darkness; and the darkness comprehended it not." John 1:4-5

There is no excuse when God sent His only begotten Son into the world because **"he lighteth every man."**

> *"That* was the true Light (Jesus), which lighteth every man that cometh into the world." John 1:9

Those who, when called by the Father, respond affirmatively in **"repentance toward God and faith toward our Lord Jesus Christ,"** will be filled with and walk in His light (Acts 20:21).

> "Then spake Jesus again unto them, saying, I am the light of the world: he that followeth me shall not walk in darkness, but shall have the light of life." John 8:12

"The Eyes of Your Understanding being En-lightened"

To be **"en-lightened"** simply means to be imbued or infused with God's light – in this case, divine light or understanding. Paul prayed this very thing for us – **"That the God of our Lord Jesus Christ, the Father of glory, may give unto you the spirit of wisdom and revelation in the knowledge of him: The eyes of your understanding being enlightened; that ye may know**

what is the hope of his calling, and what the riches of the glory of his inheritance in the saints, And what *is* the exceeding greatness of his power to usward who believe, according to the working of his mighty power." (Eph. 1:17-19)

The Greek word from which we get the word **enlightened"** here is *photizo,* from which we get the word photo. According to a Greek dictionary, the word *photizo* means *to shed rays, that is, to shine or (transitively) to brighten up (literally or figuratively): - enlighten, illuminate, (bring to, give) light, make to see.*

A photo makes one to see an image he hasn't yet seen, especially bordered by the size of the picture. When we see a photo, we are made to see the image captured in that photo – an image we would not otherwise behold. When we don't have that same photo, we are apt to forget that image. So, like Peter, to whom the Father revealed Christ, we are dependent upon the LORD to enlighten us – to give us the photo image in our hearts and minds of the Living Word, Alpha and Omega, First and the Last, King of kings, LORD of all lords, and Fountain of Living waters Himself.

> **"And Jesus answered and said unto him, Blessed art thou, Simon Bar-jona: for flesh and blood hath not revealed *it* unto thee, but my Father which is in heaven." Matthew 16:17**

With this in mind, consider the words of our LORD written in Matthew 5:8, **"Blessed *are* the pure in heart: for they shall see God."** (Matt. 5:8) Those who repent of sin and seek and obey God, will be **"pure in heart"** and able to **"see God"** and His kingdom clearly. They will be enlightened by His Spirit. Like Peter, these will be possessed by the blessed **"revelation of Jesus Christ."** (Rev. 1:1)

> **"For with thee *is* the fountain of life: in <u>thy light shall we see light</u>." Psalms 36:9**

Those who have prideful hearts, lifted up in pride concerning themselves and their own accomplishments, position, pedigree, calling, gifting, or education, instead of Jesus, cannot understand or see, and be enlightened. The LORD confounds such people (1 Cor. 1:26-31). Such is sinful vanity (Ps. 39:5).

> **"At that time Jesus answered and said, I thank thee, O Father, Lord of heaven and earth, because thou hast hid these things from the wise and prudent, and hast revealed them unto babes." Matthew 11:25**

Firstly, Jesus reveals that it is the Father's delight to reveal His light and truth to those who are humble and broken before Him – **"babes."** (See also Lk. 12:32.) Christ tells us that the Father actually hides His light from those who are puffed up in themselves in lieu of the LORD. He reveals the light of His truth to those who come to Him humbly and innocently, as little children (Matt. 11:25; 18:3-4).

> **"That no flesh should glory in his presence. But of him are ye in Christ Jesus, who of God is made unto us wisdom, and righteousness, and sanctification, and redemption: That, according as it is written, He that glorieth, let him glory in the Lord." 1 Corinthians 1:29-31**

God only opens the understanding and gives light to those who humbly obey the revealed light or truth they already have been given from Him. Consider the once rich man who died and went immediately into hell and was in torments (Lk. 16:19-31). He cried out for someone to go preach to his brothers, who were still on earth, so they would not also come to hell to be mercilessly tormented. What was God's answer? – **"And he said unto him, If they hear not Moses and the prophets, neither will they be persuaded, though one rose from the dead."** (Lk. 16:31)

Since **"the entrance of thy words giveth light"** and they had **"Moses and the prophets"** (OT Scriptures), they were accountable for the light of truth revealed therein (Ps. 119:130). This means they were accountable to their Maker and Judge and **"without excuse."** (Rom. 1:20)

"Dull of Hearing"

Hebrews 5:11

> "Search the scriptures; for in them ye think ye have eternal life: and they are they which testify of me. And <u>ye will not come to me</u>, that ye might have life." John 5:39-40

The Jewish people were actually given the Scriptures and knew them, and yet couldn't see Jesus for who He was. Since they refused to open their hearts and seek Him, they were not given the blessed revelation that Jesus was the Christ. Peter (also a Jew) was given that revelation from the Father:

> **"He (Jesus) saith unto them, But whom say ye that I am? And Simon Peter answered and said, Thou art the Christ, the Son of the living God. And Jesus answered and said unto him, Blessed art thou, Simon Bar-jona: for flesh and blood hath not revealed** *it* **unto thee, but my Father which is in heaven." Matthew 16:15-17**

The Jewish believers addressed in the book of Hebrews should have been teaching the truth, and yet they had need that someone come back and teach them the elementary/foundational principles again. Their understanding was darkened due to their inattention and refusal to obey and walk in the light of what they had previously been taught of the Word (see also Gal. 3:1; 4:19). The believers in Galatia are a prime example of how people can hear, believe, and obey the true Gospel, and then afterward be **"fallen from grace"** and need to be restored to their relationship with Christ due to erring from His truth to another gospel (Gal. 1:6-9; 5:4).

> **"Of whom we have many things to say, and hard to be uttered, seeing ye are dull of hearing. For when for the time ye ought to be teachers, ye have need that one teach you again which *be* the first principles of the oracles of God; and are become such as have need of milk, and not of strong meat." Hebrews 5:11-12**

Many today are no different than those we see in the case of Stephen's preaching to the religious (Jews), whose hearts were hardened, **"stiffnecked and uncircumcised."** They cannot hear the truth.

> **"Ye stiffnecked and uncircumcised in heart and ears, ye do always resist the Holy Ghost: as your fathers *did*, so *do* ye." Acts 7:51**

The Jews refused to believe the divine light revealed in their Scriptures, and were therefore **"dull of hearing"** – unable to understand. **"The power of darkness"** would therefore prevail over them, as it will over all who do not obey revealed truth (Lk. 22:53).

> **"For this people's heart is waxed gross, and *their* ears are dull of hearing, and their eyes they have closed; lest at any time they should see with *their* eyes, and hear with *their* ears, and should understand with *their* heart, and**

> **should be converted, and I should heal them. But blessed *are* your eyes, for they see: and your ears, for they hear." Matthew 13:15-16**

God will not give further understanding to anyone who does not obey what he already knows. To those who obey what He has shown them, He will give more light.

> **"Take heed therefore how ye hear: for whosoever hath, <u>to him shall be given; and whosoever hath not, from him shall be taken even that which he seemeth to have</u>." Luke 8:18**

There is no neutral position with the King and His kingdom. Either one is obeying the light revealed to him, or he is in jeopardy of losing that light and being turned over to **"the power of darkness."** (Lk. 22:53)

Those who shun the light of divine truth plunge headlong into spiritual darkness. All those who do not love the divinely revealed truth – the Bible – will be turned over by God Himself to a **"strong delusion"** and ultimately damned (2 Thess. 2:9-12). **"The power of darkness"** will prevail over them, even to the eternal state of **"outer darkness."** (Matt. 8:12) The light of understanding is only given by the Holy Spirit to those who **"walk in the light"** with the LORD (Ps. 25:14; Mk. 4:11; 1 Jn. 1:3, 7).

According to Holy Scripture – revealed truth – a people's **"understanding"** can be **"darkened"** when they are **"alienated from the life of God."**

> **"Having the understanding darkened, being alienated from the life of God through the ignorance that is in them, because of the blindness of their heart: Who being past feeling have given themselves over unto lasciviousness, to work all uncleanness with greediness." Ephe-**

sians 4:18-19

Here the Holy Spirit is warning these believers not to return to the rebellion of those without Christ (Gentiles), but to remember that **"ye have not so learned Christ."** (Eph. 4:20)

Of those who treasure earthly things above knowing and serving Jesus Christ, the Bible promises that **"they shall never see light."** (Ps. 49:19) Those who do not presently possess the light/understanding of the King and His eternal kingdom, are darkened and will go to eternal darkness. In contrast, those who love Him who is the **"light of the world"** have been given His light now, and will bask in the glory of it for all eternity (Ps. 36:9; Jn. 8:12; Rev. 21:23-24; 22:5). Jesus promised that all who know Him – **"the light of the world"** – **"shall not walk in darkness, but shall have the light of life."** (Jn. 8:12)

The LORD rejoices to reveal His covenant truths and blessed promises to those who fear Him.

> **"The secret of the LORD *is* with them that fear him; and he will show them his covenant." Psalms 25:14**

God be praised that His holy light dispels all darkness – in our understanding, present spiritual state, and in eternity!

Concerning those who live in His holy light, the LORD says this:

> **"But know that the LORD hath set apart him that is godly for himself: the LORD will hear when I call unto him. Stand in awe, and sin not: commune with your own heart upon your bed, and be still. Selah. Offer the sacrifices of**

> **righteousness, and put your trust in the LORD. *There be* many that say, Who will show us *any* good? LORD, lift thou up the light of thy countenance upon us. Thou hast put gladness in my heart, more than in the time *that* their corn and their wine increased. I will both lay me down in peace, and sleep: for thou, LORD, only makest me dwell in safety." Psalms 4:3-8**

Jesus Christ, **"the light of the world,"** makes His face to shine upon those who have repented and believed upon Him and are living in His holy light (Jn. 8:12).

> **"The LORD bless thee, and keep thee: The LORD make his face shine upon thee, and be gracious unto thee: The LORD lift up his countenance upon thee, and give thee peace." Numbers 6:24-26**

The Promise of Eternal Light
Christ will reign supreme with His beloved people forever. As contrasted with the **"outer darkness"** to be forever experienced by the wicked, there will be no darkness in His eternal abode. All darkness shall be expelled by Him who is **"the light."** (Jn. 8:12) Jesus Christ is the light to His people now, and will forever be their light. The light brings a myriad of blessings, including the dispelling of all darkness, and the bestowing of eternal warmth, sight, and joy!

> **"And I saw no temple therein: for the Lord God Almighty and the Lamb are the temple of it. And the city had no need of the sun, neither of the moon, to shine in it: for the glory of God did lighten it, and the Lamb *is* the light thereof. And the nations of them which are saved shall walk in the light of it ..." Revelation 21:22-24**

PRAYER: *Father, forgive my sin for not honoring You first and foremost in my personal life. Unite my heart to fear Thy holy name. I declare my iniquity of idolatry and spiritual adultery this moment, asking You to forgive my sins and take fresh possession of my whole being. Right now, if never before, and regardless of any past spiritual experience or state, I ask You to flood and fill my whole being and faculties. Jesus, I now bow before You and beg You to make Thy holy face to shine upon me. Bless me to know and fear You from this moment forward. I am all Yours, Jesus! Enlighten my eyes to see Thy everlasting truth and soon coming kingdom. In Jesus' name. Amen.*

Capture Points

- According to Jesus, what happens to those who don't presently walk in the divine.

- light they have been given? John 12:35.

- On an index card, transcribe the words of Christ recorded in John 8:12 (KJV).

- recommended). Personally recording Holy Scripture is the way to get it into one's mind and heart, so as to be able to meditate upon it and memorize it.

- Meditate upon and discuss who the Bible defines as a **"babe,"** and who it defines.

- as a mature or **"full age"** believer. Hebrews 5:11-14

Chapter Seven

The Cross, Hearing, and Speaking

> **"For there must be also heresies among you, that they which are approved may be made manifest among you." 1 Corinthians 11:19**

We see in this verse of a truth that **"heresies"** have a place in God's overall economy of things as pertains to His justice in dealing with men. Every person is given the choice (Deut. 30:19; Josh. 24:15; Prov. 1:29; Isa. 1:18-20; Rom. 6:16; Rev. 22:17). Those who do not choose to fear Him and therefore love His truth, are sent by Him a **"strong delusion."**

> **"And with all deceivableness of unrighteousness in them that perish; <u>because</u> they received not the love of the truth, that they**

> **might be saved. And for this cause God shall send them strong delusion, that they should believe a lie: That they all might be damned who believed not the truth, but had pleasure in unrighteousness." 2 Thessalonians 2:10-12**

First deception, then delusion, and ultimately unending **"damnation"** is the final result to be reaped by all who do not choose to foster in their lives a love for their Creator's truth.

Eternal life, divine revelation, understanding, and insight are granted to all who are in Christ. The insight (understanding) of Heaven is given to those who humble themselves and follow Christ, who is the truth - just as He prescribed in His Word (Matt. 11:25; 1 Cor. 2:9-16). This relationship begins when the individual hears the voice of God calling him to repentance and responds obediently (Jn. 6:44; Acts 3:19). The called person must choose to follow Jesus by denying himself and taking up his cross – dethroning himself and putting God first in his life (Matt. 16:24-25).

The Reason Heresies and Deceivers Prosper

Below are listed two of the reasons fad books become bestsellers, heresies thrive, beguilers flourish, and deception prospers exponentially among millions who claim to be Christians. For these same reasons, millions who claim to be saved will not be ready and admitted into Christ's kingdom when the Bridegroom returns:

Reason 1:

> So many want some man to tell them what their "purpose" is, because they claim to know Jesus and are still running around life confused. Why? Because they have thus far refused to seek His holy face for themselves, pouring over His words

and seeking Him in prayer communion. They are therefore empty and still void of any revelation and understanding as to foundational truths revealed in Holy Scripture – like who Jesus really is, why God created man, what went wrong between God and mankind, why Jesus came to the earth, etc. You see, it is only in going to GOD Himself – the One who created us and died for our sins – that one will ever understand his divinely-given purpose. What is that purpose? It is to glorify our Maker by following Christ in His Gospel – dying, being buried deep with Him in death to self, and seeing His holy hand of power resurrect us to glorify Him!

Reason 2:

Regrettably and astoundingly, one can observe that the vast majority of people in leadership in this late hour refuse to point people to the Source; they would rather BE the source! They refuse to lay down their own lives and thereby be instruments of Jesus to build His true Church as they point people to Him alone – to His Word and their need to know it themselves and to seek God in prayer fervently and perpetually. These are hirelings and **"IDOL shepherds,"** and by them there has been induced on the earth **"famine in the land, not a famine of bread, nor a thirst for water, but of hearing the words of the LORD."** (Zech. 11:17; Amos 8:11) As He warned us all, many of God's people have already waxed cold in their hearts, leaving their **"first love,"** and are forfeiting their relationship and eternity with Him due to being **"destroyed for lack of knowledge."** (Hos. 4:6; Matt. 24:10-13; Rev. 2:4-5) Any man in leadership who is not teaching people that they need JESUS and not *him,* and is not teaching them to **"seek ye**

out of the book of the Lord (for yourself) and read," is a self-serving, vile and venomous wolf! (Isa. 34:16; Col. 2:18-19; 2 Tim. 2:15) Due to personal rebellion and the epidemic of wolves, men are void of the understanding of their own need to draw nigh to the LORD in repentance and seek the face of the LORD for themselves, putting Jesus first in all things as they lay down their lives that He might reign in and through them (Lk. 9:23-24; 13:3, 5; 14:33).

The Glorious 66!

While driving my car recently I was listening to a radio program that airs every morning for 3 hours. The host reads from another man's book. He narrates man's words to his large listening audience, which listens and apparently does not object. I suspect that those who are blessed to be brought into the light by the truth, cannot bear or do not have ears for such. As usual, what he was reading from a mere man's book was conjecture, human philosophy, foolish psychology, and reasoning, etc. Whatever happened to God's Word? Where did the Holy Scriptures disappear to? Where are those who are zealous for the LORD and therefore His holy words?! What about God's glorious 66 books?! This man and so many others today, have displaced God's words for those inferior and temporal reasonings, philosophies, theories, and rationalisms of mere sinful men.

Colossians 2:8 says:

> **"Beware lest any man spoil you through philosophy and vain deceit, after the tradition of men, after the rudiments of the world, and not after Christ."**

Those who migrate to the words and philosophies of mere men, esteeming them higher than the words of God, demonstrate that they are idolaters and **"savourest not the things that be of God, but those that be of men."** (Matt. 16:23; Ezek. 14:3; Jn. 5:39-44) Jesus draws a conclusion concerning those who **"savourest not the things that be of God, but those that be of men."** He infers that they are of **"Satan."** (Matt. 16:23)

The Son of God says of religionists that they will not come to Him, even though they are zealous of their religion and its beliefs (Mk. 7:6-10; Jn. 5:39-44).

Always remember that true disciples have an ear for God's words, and like Paul the apostle, all obedient and faithful messengers of the LORD are mere conduits of His Spirit and truth, so that men's affections and faith **"should not stand in the wisdom of men, but in the power of God."** (1 Cor. 2:1-5; 2 Cor. 4:7)

> **"And he said unto me, Son of man, go, get thee unto the house of Israel, and <u>speak with MY WORDS unto them</u>." Ezekiel 3:4**

We see clearly in this passage, that when God sends a man to speak to His people, He sends that man to speak GOD's words and not his own or anyone else's words or message!

> **"<u>If any man speak, let him speak as the oracles of God</u>; if any man minister, let him do it as of the ability which God giveth: that God in all things may be glorified through Jesus Christ, to whom be praise and dominion for ever and ever. Amen." 1 Peter 4:11**

The Bible tells us that Jesus will reward those who love and serve Him (instead of self) faithfully. They will be blessed now and forever with His joy – **"His lord said** unto him, Well done, good and faithful servant; thou hast been faithful over a few things, I will make thee ruler over many things: enter thou into the joy of thy lord."** (Matt. 25:23)

> **"As the cold of snow in the time of harvest, so is <u>a faithful messenger</u> to them that send him: for he refresheth the soul of his masters." Proverbs 25:13**

The Master Jesus is well pleased at all the **"faithful messenger(s)"** who obey Him by letting Him speak for Himself, as they simply communicate the **"preserve(d)"** and **"purified"** words of holy truth (Ps. 12:6-7; Prov. 30:5).

Jesus said of the Word of God, **"Thy word is truth,"** and so we know God's words and truth are synonymous – they are one (Jn. 17:17). There is no need to search the Universe for the truth – God has already given it to man in Jesus Christ and in the Holy Scriptures. God's Word is divine wisdom, truth, and His perfect will. Those who know Him embrace Him who is **"the way, the truth, and the life"** and communicate those things (Jn. 14:6; 17:17).

> **"He that speaketh truth sheweth forth righteousness: but a false witness deceit." Proverbs 12:17**

Did you catch that truth? Read the verse above again please. Those who speak God's Word show it forth or display it, while those who speak any other message are false witnesses – they are full of deceit that the LORD desires to circumcise or cut away out of their hearts.

> "And is it not obvious that, just as it is a crime to disturb the peace when truth reigns, it is also a crime to remain at peace when the truth is being

destroyed? ... Weaklings are those who know the truth, but maintain it only (when) in their interest to do so, and (otherwise) forsake it." Blaise Pascal

The crucified disciple migrates toward and acquiesces toward divine truth, while shunning and despising that which is contrary (Ps. 119:104, 128; Isa. 8:20). His heart has been and is being circumcised to hear God's words, as he has and continues to **"buy the truth and sell it not."** (Prov. 23:23) His heart says with Paul, **"Let God be true and every man a liar."** (Rom. 3:4) He embraces what Jesus stated concerning His words – **"the scripture cannot be broken."** (Jn. 10:35) Like Jeremiah, members of the **"little flock"** of the Father seek out and devour the words of their LORD (Lk. 12:32):

> **"Thy words were found, and I did eat them; and thy word was unto me the joy and rejoicing of mine heart: for I am called by thy name, O LORD God of hosts." Jeremiah 15:16**

Christ's saints value His truth. It is more important than their **"necessary food."** (Job 23:12)

> **"Neither have I gone back from the commandment of his lips; I have esteemed the words of his mouth more than my necessary food." Job 23:12**

The LORD is pleased to grant **"ears to hear"** to those who participate with Him in the process of circumcision of their hearts (Phil. 3:3; 2 Tim. 4:2-4; Rev. 2-3).

> **"Ye stiffnecked and uncircumcised in heart and ears, ye do always resist the Holy Ghost: as your fathers did, so do ye." Acts 7:51**

The religious person, who is hardened by sinful pride and is therefore **"stiffnecked and uncircumcised in**

heart and ears," has no appetite for the Word. Those who are genuinely **"born again"** by the **"incorruptible seed"** of **"the word of God," "have tasted (experienced)"** and seen **"that the Lord is gracious."** These invariably delight in and **"desire the sincere (pure) milk of the word."**

> **"Being born again, not of corruptible seed, but of incorruptible, by the word of God, which liveth and abideth for ever ... As newborn babes, desire the sincere milk of the word, that ye may grow thereby: If so be ye have tasted that the Lord is gracious." 1 Peter 1:23; 2:2-3**

"Affections"

According to the divine economy, in order to locate where we stand with Christ, we need not look any further than our appetites, affections, and *what* we have ears to hear.

> **"And they that are Christ's <u>have</u> crucified the flesh with the affections and lusts." Galatians 5:24**

"They that are Christ's" have the **"affections"** of their hearts set upon Jesus and the things and work that pertains to His kingdom, and not the things of this sinful world system (Jn. 4:27; James 4:4; 1 Jn. 2:14-17). They migrate to and delight in meditating upon and talking about Christ by communing in His wonderful Word (Josh. 1:8; Ps. 1:1-2; Col. 3:16). Those who are not born again, or are not presently abiding in relationship with Jesus, find no pleasure in His words or in talking about Him. Concerning those who do not remain in Christ (remain saved after being saved), Jesus told us that they will be **"cast forth as a branch, and ... withered; and men gather them, and cast them into the fire, and they are burned."** (Jn. 15:6) They are carnal and cannot please God.

> "**For they that are after the flesh do mind the things of the flesh; but they that are after the Spirit the things of the Spirit. For <u>to be carnally minded is death;</u> but to be spiritually minded is life and peace. Because the carnal mind is enmity against God: for it is not subject to the law of God, neither indeed can be. So then they that are in the flesh cannot please God." Romans 8:5-8**
>
> Note: **"For they that are after the flesh do mind the things of the flesh; but they that are after the Spirit the things of the Spirit."** This is how we can test whether or not we are of God or against Christ (Matt. 6:24; 12:30). One's verbal profession has no bearing on such, especially if there is not clear fruit or outward works to prove that there is a soul-saving relationship with Christ (Matt. 3:7-10; Tit. 1:16; James 2).

The person who is not hungering for more of Christ, is not devouring His Word, does not have a prayer life, and does not financially support the ministry, is clearly not walking with God. The fruit of his life plainly reveals that he is what the LORD terms "**carnally minded,**" and is therefore abiding in spiritual **"death"** – separation from God. This person should either repent fully or just go live it up because he is hell bound in his current condition.

When one belongs to Christ, the fruit of his life testifies of that fact clearly with what he does and where his focus is – on heavenly things, rather than on earthly (Matt. 6:19-21; Phil. 3:18-21).

> **"They profess that they know God; but in works they deny him, being abominable, and disobedient, and unto every good work reprobate." Titus 1:16**

Without exception, the person who is given over to the LORD is given over to His cause. What concerns God concerns him. His finances and heart are behind Christ's Gospel (Matt. 6:19-21). He is about his Father's business and not his own (Lk. 2:49). What business the LORD declared and demonstrated to be important, is important to the truly saved person.

> **"So likewise, whosoever he be of you that forsaketh not all that he hath, he cannot be my disciple." Luke 14:33**

There's a simple fruit-checker to see if we are walking in the Spirit or in the flesh – if we mind His things, we are of Him, and if we don't, we aren't. The mind which sets its affections upon the LORD is a mind filled with energy, will, and work toward what is important to Him. The man with such a mind is kept in **"perfect peace,"** because he is presenting himself a living sacrifice to the LORD, and his mind is set upon things above and not on the things of the earth (Rom. 12:1-2; Col. 3:1-4).

> **"Thou wilt keep him in perfect peace, whose mind is stayed on thee: because he trusteth in thee." Isaiah 26:3**

> In contrast, those who have their minds set upon the things of this world prove they are serving themselves and not the LORD.
> **"(For many walk, of whom I have told you often, and now tell you even weeping, that they are the <u>enemies of the cross of Christ</u>. Whose end is destruction (hell), whose God is their belly (carnal, self-serving appetites), and whose glory is in their shame, <u>who mind earthly things</u>.)" Philippians 3:18-19**

Those who have been and are being circumcised in heart, as they are daily and perpetually **"crucified with**

Christ," turn away from and expose lies, and they have **"ears"** for and a love for divine truth given to us in the written Word. The affections of their hearts are set upon Christ and His coming and everlasting kingdom, and not on the things of this sin-cursed world. They are therefore busy dying, that His power and grace might reign in them to the cutting away of anything in their lives that does not bring God glory.

> **"If ye then be risen with Christ, seek those things which are above, where Christ sitteth on the right hand of God. Set your affection on things above, not on things on the earth. For ye are dead, and your life is hid with Christ in God. When Christ, who is our life, shall appear, then shall ye also appear with him in glory. Mortify therefore your members which are upon the earth; fornication, uncleanness, inordinate affection, evil concupiscence, and covetousness, which is idolatry." Colossians 3:1-5**

Only the work of the Holy Spirit, through the inner working of the cross, can bring about the sanctified life which includes upward affections and a circumcised, broken, contrite, humble heart of flesh that responds perfectly and delightfully to the voice and words of the Savior (Ps. 4:3; 40:8; 1 Jn. 5:3).

> **"For thus saith the LORD to the men of Judah and Jerusalem, <u>Break up your fallow ground</u>, and <u>sow not among thorns</u>. <u>Circumcise yourselves to the LORD</u>, and <u>take away the foreskins of your heart</u>, ye men of Judah and inhabitants of Jerusalem: lest my fury come forth like fire, and burn that none can quench it, because of the evil of your doings ... O Jerusalem, <u>wash thine heart from wickedness</u>, that thou mayest be saved. How long shall thy vain**

thoughts lodge within thee?" Jeremiah 4:3-4, 14

Circumcision involves the cutting away and removal of that which is excess. It was the sign of the covenant of the LORD with His people Israel, and is also the sign or fruit of His work in all of His people today.

> **"For he is not a Jew, which is one outwardly; neither is that circumcision, which is outward in the flesh: But he is a Jew, which is one inwardly; and <u>circumcision is that of the heart</u>, in the spirit, and not in the letter; whose praise is not of men, but of God." Romans 2:28-29**

What was *physical* under the Old Covenant, is *spiritual* under the New.

All whom He saves are *positionally* crucified with Christ and yet must buy into and participate in the Gospel by dying, being buried, and trusting and allowing God to raise them up. We who have been born again have been crucified with Christ and circumcised inwardly and are to follow suit **"daily"** in this crucified life (Lk. 9:23-24; Rom. 6:3-7; Gal. 2:20; 5:24).

According to the above passage from the prophet Jeremiah, **"vain thoughts"** must be taken away or circumcised from the hearts of God's people.

If a person does not hear God's Word, it is clear that they are not His – they are not set apart by Him in salvation and for His use.

> **"He that is <u>of God</u> heareth God's words: ye therefore hear them not, because ye are <u>not of God</u>." John 8:47**

Here Christ makes it crystal clear that those **"of God heareth God's words"** and those **"not of God"** refuse to hear, embrace, and do them. Those who steer away from God's Word, do not get into it for themselves, and have no hunger for it are simply **"not of God"** according to the Almighty Himself. Jesus told us that those who are ashamed of Him or of His words are not of Him, and will not be going to Heaven (Mk. 8:38).

Jesus told us that **"God is a Spirit,"** and if a person does not worship Him **"in spirit and in truth,"** it is because that person does not know Him. Christ said that this was a **"must"** – essential.

> **"But the hour cometh, and now is, when <u>the true worshippers shall worship the Father in spirit and in truth</u>: for the Father seeketh such to worship him. <u>God is a Spirit: and they that worship him MUST worship him in spirit and in truth</u>." John 4:23-24**

The only way that an individual can be saved and serve God **"in spirit and in truth,"** is to be **"born again."** (Jn. 3:1-8; Tit. 3:5-6; 1 Pet. 1:23) When he is born again and continues abiding in Jesus, he will worship God in the Spirit and have no confidence in the flesh or the fleshly things of mere men.

> **"For we are the circumcision, which worship God in the spirit, and rejoice in Christ Jesus, and have no confidence in the flesh." Philippians 3:3**

It is only when the cross of Christ has had its way in circumcising a man's heart that he can delight in God.

> **"I delight to do thy will, O my God: yea, thy law (Word) is within my heart." Psalms 40:8**

The cross and its mortifying of the sinful nature separates the heart from carnality, hardness, deceit, filthiness, and self-will, allowing it to hear clearly and respond obediently (Jer. 4:3-4, 14; Ezek. 36:26; Hos. 10:12; Acts 15:9; Rom. 8:13-14; 1 Cor. 1:18; 2 Cor. 7:1; Heb. 3:12-15; 13:9).

Those whose hearts are full of *self* instead of the *Savior*, **"heap to themselves teachers, having itching ears ... And ... turn away their ears from the truth."** (2 Tim. 4:3) These who have a mere **"form of godliness"** and are **"lovers of their own selves,"** help fulfill the foretold multiplicity of deceivers in this last hour – **"Evil men and seducers shall wax worse and worse."** (2 Tim. 3:13)

> **"Preach the word; be instant in season, out of season; reprove, rebuke, exhort with all longsuffering and doctrine. For the time will come when they will not endure sound doctrine; but after their own lusts shall they heap to themselves teachers, having itching ears; And they shall turn away their ears from the truth, and shall be turned unto fables." 2 Timothy 4:2-4**

All who do not communicate His pure Word are false teachers, and they only find place with those whose hearts are not given over to Christ (2 Tim. 4:3-4; Heb. 13:9). His **"faithful messenger(s)"** are joyfully overflowing with the **"treasures"** He has deposited in their **"earthen vessels,"** and their cups run/spill over onto those they serve with the Gospel (Ps. 23:5; 2 Cor. 4:7).

The Psalmist prayed thus concerning evil communicators who spawn and propagate heresies that lead people away from Jesus:

> **"Let not an evil speaker be established in the earth ... " Psalms 140:11**

It's only as men are not circumcised in heart and ear

that they allow, endorse, enable, and cause false prophets to prosper.

Only dead men, who are in their personal lives preferring the LORD above themselves, can and will contain the life of Christ and speak His holy words faithfully. Many today who hold positions of leadership and influence, simply do not want to die.

> "The flesh, smiling and confident, preaches and sings about the cross; before that cross it bows and toward that cross it points with carefully staged histrionics – but upon that cross it will not die, and the reproach of that cross it stubbornly refuses to bear." A.W. Tozer, *The Divine Conquest*

It's only misled men who mislead men. Misled men are men who deny the daily cross Christ commanded us to take up (Lk. 9:23-24). Un-crucified men will deny Christ by delivering a message different from the one He delivered.

> "... A third defect in our message is our tendency to keep the terms of discipleship hidden until a decision has been made for Jesus. Our Lord never did this. The message He preached included the cross as well as the crown ... We popularize the message and promise fun. The result of all this is that we have people believing without knowing what they believe (with) no doctrinal basis for their decision. They do not know the implications of commitment to Christ. They have never experienced the mysterious, miraculous work of the Holy Spirit in regeneration." (Author's emphasis) William MacDonald, "Evangelical Dilemma," *Milk & Honey*, 4/07, p. 4

It's only as we cry out for Him to **"increase"** and as we ourselves **"decrease,"** that Christ's power, life, and message can reign in our mortal bodies (Jn. 3:30; 2 Co. 4:10-12). Only those whose lives are laid down can possibly be *raised up* by Him to be used of Him, and they by His divine **"ability"** make Jesus known – **"that God in all things may be glorified through Jesus Christ."**

Do we have ears to hear **"what the Spirit saith unto the churches"** in this late hour? (Rev. 2-3) It's only as we are flattened, prostrate, and bowed down before His Majesty that He will elevate us in His power, wisdom, and grace (divine ability) to know Him and to be used of Him. We are not worthy to be saved into His family or used of Him, and without Christ, we **"can do nothing."** (Jn. 15:5; Tit. 3:5-6).

Are you truly **"crucified with Christ"**?

> **"I am crucified with Christ: nevertheless I live; yet not I, but Christ liveth in me: and the life which I now live in the flesh I live by the faith of the Son of God, who loved me, and gave himself for me." Galatians 2:20**

Be it known that only crucified men can glorify God and only crucified men do not mislead others, nor do they follow false prophets who are the enemies of Christ and the cross of Christ. They have ears to hear and a heart to faithfully embrace the words of the One they love supremely – Jesus Christ.

PRAYER: *Father, please break me to powder. Crush me that I might be abased in Thy holy presence and thereby preserved of You. Grant a teachable and contrite heart, Holy Father. Give me a heart after You and ears to hear what You would say to Your people in this late hour. I love You, Jesus, and thank You for dying to mediate between God and men. I am crucified with Christ and nevertheless I live, yet not I, but Christ that lives in me, and the life which I now live in the flesh, I live by the faith of the Son* *of God, who loved me and gave Himself for me. In Jesus' name. Amen.*

Capture Points

- Discuss in detail what divine truth is being conveyed to us in 1 Corinthians 11:19. As usual, remember to bring in other passages (Isa. 28:9-10; 1 Cor. 2:13; 2 Cor. 13:1).

- *Carefully and prayerfully write out Colossians 2:8 on an index card.*

- Prayerfully and biblically talk about 2 Timothy 4:2-5.

SafeGuardYourSoul.com

Chapter Eight

The Only Way Up is Down

The Up and Down Principal of God's Kingdom

> "And the remnant that is escaped of the house of Judah shall again <u>take root DOWNWARD, and bear fruit UPWARD</u>." Isaiah 37:31

Father, please bless each of us to learn the cross - the way of Christ's cross. We know it is only then that Your blessed resurrection grace and power will raise us upward to bring glory to Your holy name.

> "The One who is the Highest came to become the lowest. We who are the lowest, seek to be the highest." Unknown

Have you seen the book titles being peddled of late to Christians? The Christian market is considerably large in size, so many beguilers are farming it to sell their wares. But are they Christ and cross-centered or self-centered? Think about the titles we see of late. See if you can see the sharp contrast between the teachings of today's wolves and the teachings of Christ and His apostles (Acts 2:42). Put on your Scriptural mindset – the mind of Christ – and compare the following. Today's bestselling "Christian" titles speak of:

> Repositioning yourself and living life without limits (by your own doing and as your own "little god," doing your own bidding apart from God and being crucified with Christ)

> Living your best life now in this short-lived life and sinful world (instead of living the cross and letting God lay up His treasures and reward in the coming world)

> Getting all you can in this world (yet the LORD tells us that if we love this world, His love is not in us)

> Daring to dream big dreams (whose dreams?)

> Moving up (instead of down into Christ's death and burial)

> Soaring upward (with no mention of the crucified life)

> Living a sensational life (without Jesus? While disobeying His command to die that He might raise you up?)

> Divine destiny (outside of the message of the cross, an illicit, sinful soul power divorced from knowing the LORD in the fellowship of His suffer-

ings while being made conformable to His death)

Becoming a better you (a message that completely ignores the Bible truth of our utter sinful depravity and need to be crucified with Christ – so this message is built upon an unsalvageable foundation)

Creating the life you want (instead of being broken, humble, and fully dependent upon the LORD, allowing Him to lead your life and to make out of it what He desires)

Reaching your full potential (another message to allure masses to worship at the altar of self in the total absence of the message of Christ, which calls all men everywhere to repent and return from all idolatry to the LORD and the life of the cross)

Discovering God's purpose for your life (driven by purpose, or crucified and led by His Word and Holy Spirit? Spirit-led or led by the self-serving desire for a purpose? God's purpose or man's? More sinful and self-serving fruit emanating out of the uncircumcised hearts of those who would seek purpose in place of dying to self, and letting Him reveal His holy purpose through His Word and Spirit)

Loving your life (Jesus said that all those who will enter His eternal kingdom must hate their own lives in this world - Lk. 14:26)

Have you seen books like this that entice consumers to indulge in the self-life instead of living the crucified life?

There is a current book out, the title of which proclaims that the reader should love his own life. In diametrical opposition, Jesus told us that if **"any man"** does not **"hate ... his own life,"** he **"cannot be my disciple."**

Whom will we trust? Whom will you believe? Whom will we follow? Whose message will we obey?

> **"If any man come to me, and hate not his father, and mother, and wife, and children, and brethren, and sisters, yea, and <u>his own life</u> also, he cannot be my disciple. And whosoever doth not bear his cross, and come after me, cannot be my disciple. For which of you, intending to build a tower, sitteth not down first, and counteth the cost, whether he have sufficient to finish it? Lest haply, after he hath laid the foundation, and is not able to finish it, all that behold it begin to mock him, Saying, This man began to build, and was not able to finish." Luke 14:26-30**

According to the Son of God, are we to learn to love or hate our lives in this fleeting world?

It has been wisely stated that "a person can be known by his library" or by "the company he keeps." When you view your own or someone else's library, you may be able to get a scope of that person's heart and the focus of his life. You will see whose heart that person's ear is bowed down to hear. Those who love Jesus will be purists – loving His holy truth supremely (KJV Bible). If they choose to read extra-biblical books, these books will have been written by authors who speak **"as of the oracles of God."** (1 Pet. 4:11)

In most cases unwittingly, those who purchase these books are accessories to the crime and travesty of misleading souls (Isa. 9:16; Ezek. 22:25-27). They render aid to false teachers by funding their folly, which misrepresents and defies Christ (2 Chron. 19:2; Prov. 17:15; 24:24; 2 Jn. 7-11).

Regrettably, in the vast majority of messages given by "Christian" leaders, one can observe that there is no mention of dying to self, personal holiness, taking up the cross, fearing God, looking for Christ's soon return, mortifying the deeds of the body, etc. These essential and eternally consequential messages from Christ and His holy apostles don't sell books in large volumes, and make men "Christian celebrities." In order to sell books, supposed Christian pastors have forsaken the LORD and divine truth to become successful in this passing and sinful world. They utilize tantalizing titles and themes that **"allure through the lusts of the flesh,"** calling people to worship at the altar of self (2 Pet. 2:18). Make no mistake, beloved; these are the very false prophets of the final days we are so often warned of by the Holy Spirit in God's holy Word (Matt. 7:15-23; 24:3-5, 11, 24; 1 Tim. 4:1-3; 2 Tim. 3:13; 4:3-5; 2 Pet. 2:1-3; 1 Jn. 4:1).

The remnant of God's people are a **"little flock"** characterized by their participation in the true and original Gospel, which concerns death, burial, and resurrection, and the life of Christ manifesting gloriously in the life of His beloved people (Lk. 12:32; Acts 1-28; 1 Cor. 15:1-4; 2 Cor. 4:10-12). Look around you, and only as you see and observe a person who is putting himself aside – dying – will you see the true Gospel in **"the operation of God."** (Col. 2:12) The resurrecting **"operation of God"** begins when the individual dies and is buried. This is where you are going to see the working of the Spirit in power, propelling His people to be fruitful in the work of the Gospel (see book of Acts). He who **"raised"** up Jesus from that grave, also just as certainly raises up all those who are bowed down humbly at His Majesty (Ps. 145:14; Col. 2:12).

> **"Buried with him in baptism, wherein also ye are risen with him through the faith of the operation of God, who hath raised him from the**

dead." Colossians 2:12

The Gospel and Its Work

Most who claim to know Christ have ignored His command to "**deny**" self and take up the cross, which is a prerequisite for following Him (Matt. 16:23-24; Mk. 8:34-38; Lk. 9:23-24).

Jesus said that **"narrow is the way, which leadeth unto life, and <u>few</u> there be that find it."** He promised that those who will enter into Heaven through **"the straight gate"** are **"few"** (Matt. 7:13-14). The Son of God also said that **"the labourers are <u>few</u>"** when referring to Gospel workers (Matt. 9:37). From this observation, can we not draw the conclusion that those who are truly saved have the fruit of obedience manifesting in their personal lives, and such obedience includes co-laboring with Him in bringing in "**his harvest**"? Can we not also conclude that those who are disobedient will be those who will hear from Him, on Judgment Day, **"depart from me"**? (Matt. 7:21-23; 25:41; Lk. 13:27; Tit. 1:16)

Christ told us that **"whosoever"** would **"follow"** Him must **"deny himself and take up his cross,"** not only for Him but also for **"the gospel."** (Mk. 8:35) *Any person not actively involved in the work of the Gospel should seriously consider whether or not he is truly saved.* It would appear that that person is denying Christ instead of self, and this is why he is **"ashamed"** of Him, and is therefore not confessing Him (Mk. 8:38; Lk. 12:7-8).

Christ promised that it is the **"Father's good pleasure"** to give His remnant, or **"little flock,"** His kingdom – now and eternally. And throughout the record of Holy Writ we have of **"the thoughts of his heart,"** we see that He lifts up those whose lives are obediently laid down in the death of the self-life (Ps. 33:11). These bow downward, sinking down deep into His death and burial, and He raises them upward in rich fruitfulness to His glory. This resurrection living is enabled by the Holy Spirit and the individual's willingness and obedience to lose his own life by falling down into the ground and dying (Ps. 145:14; Isa. 37:31; Jn. 12:24). As the disciple does so, the killing power of the Holy Spirit takes over and anoints him to the burial of self, while raising him upward in fruitful living – resurrection living.

> "The cross has a killing power that the flesh cannot stand against – not by human effort – 'through the Spirit.'" Travis Bryan III

The disciple is not alone. He is the very **"temple of the Holy Ghost,"** and not his own, but rather **"bought with a price"** in order that he might **"glorify God."**

> **"What? know ye not that your body is the temple of the Holy Ghost which is in you, which ye have of God, and <u>ye are not your own? For ye are bought with a price</u>: therefore glorify God in your body, and in your spirit, which are God's." 1 Corinthians 6:19-20**

Lest one should feel he himself is worthy or capable of pleasing God, it should be understood that it is the divine Person of the Holy Spirit, resident and at work in every true believer, that makes this all possible.

> **"For if ye live after the flesh, ye shall die: but if ye through the Spirit do mortify the deeds of the body, ye shall live." Romans 8:13**

It is **"through the Spirit"** that the life of crucifixion is resurrected and enabled. This comes only as the disciple participates in the Gospel by dying to self, being buried with Christ, and being raised up in divine power.

Many want to be used of God – to be full of His Spirit

and doing His work. Yet in our day, as in every generation, only a few are willing to **"take root downward"** that they might be **"raised up"** in His power, grace, and blessing to bring forth **"the fruit of the Spirit,"** and blessed to do His work among His people and in evangelizing lost souls (Isa. 37:31; Rom. 8:11; 2 Cor. 4:14; Gal. 5:22-23).

Is the LORD manifesting in your life **"the fruit of the Spirit"**? (Gal. 5:22-23) If not, it is because He is not in you, and you are separated from Him due to sin. Galatians 5:19-21 cites 17 sins which will separate one from the LORD, and these are "**the works of the flesh.**"

If His death doesn't work in me, neither will His life. I must be buried with Him – dead to self-will, waiving all of my rights – that He might raise me up to please and glorify Him. The only way up truly is down. *Father, please teach us Your Gospel – teach us Your way!*

I cannot be filled with or used of Him if I choose to live unto myself – to live this life as my own god, sitting on the throne of my own heart, while making all my own decisions as my own lord. No, in order to be filled with His precious presence and used of Him, I must die and be buried with Him (Rom. 6:3-4). First, I must experience His death in order to experience His resurrection life.

"Raised up Jesus from the dead" (Rom. 8:11) – Jesus had to first be dead, to die, before He could be raised up. The same is true for us – we must first be dead to self in order for God to fill us with His Holy Spirit of power and raise us up to bring glory to Him.

The volume of fruit borne upward will always be consistent with the depth of death and burial I allow to occur by the enabling power of the Holy Ghost, and my own willingness to submit to the crucified life. The height of the tree is determined by the depth of its roots. Deep roots stabilize the visible tree, which is seen because it protrudes upward on the earth toward Heaven.

The Scriptures follow a pattern of death and resurrection, a downward death and upward life. See if you can observe such a truth in the following verses:

> **"The LORD upholdeth all that fall, and <u>raiseth UP all *those that be* bowed DOWN</u>." Psalms 145:14**

Do you possess the blessed desire to be raised up by the Almighty? When He raises us up, it will be by His power and blessing, and these benefits will then be resident in our daily lives. According to His divine wisdom given us in His precious Precepts, in order to be **"raised up"** one must first be **"bowed down."** The LORD will not raise up any person who is still alive in his own power - He only raises up **"those that be bowed down"** in sincere humility before His majesty (Ps. 145:14; Jn. 12:23-25; Rom. 8:11).

> **"Those that be bowed down"** will be flattened and **"take root downward,"** and be raised up in blessed fruitfulness (Isa. 37:31).

> **"Thou fool, that which thou sowest is not quickened (made alive), except it die." 1 Corinthians 15:36**

According to God's Word, we are fools if we believe that God is going to raise up something that is not dead – **"except it die."** Jesus says:

> **"Verily, verily, I say unto you, Except a corn (grain) of wheat fall into the ground and die, it abideth alone: but if it die, it bringeth forth much fruit." John 12:24**

In order to **"bear fruit upward,"** one must *first* be planted in the house (kingdom) of the LORD and **"take root downward"** in the rich soil of His truth. The resurrection life of Jesus and ample fruitfulness will be the result.

> **"And whosoever shall exalt himself (upward) shall be abased (humbled); and he that shall humble himself shall be exalted." Matthew 23:12**

> **"He must INCREASE, but I *must* DECREASE." John 3:30**

> **"And Jesus answered them, saying, The hour is come, that the Son of man should be glorified. Verily, verily, I say unto you, Except a corn of wheat FALL INTO THE GROUND (downward) and die, it abideth alone: but if it die, it bringeth forth much fruit (upward). He that loveth his life shall lose it; and he that hateth his life (downward) in this world shall keep it unto life eternal (upward)." John 12:23-25**

> **"Humble yourselves (downward heart posture) in the sight of the Lord, and he shall lift you UP." James 4:10**

The life of Christ will raise a man upward, and this is after that man bows down his life or humbles himself under the mighty hand of God – first at initial salvation, and then in the consecrated life that brings God glory (Matt. 18:3-4).

> **"But he giveth more grace. Wherefore he saith, God resisteth the proud, but giveth grace unto the humble." James 4:6**

The LORD tells us here that He **"giveth grace (divine enablement) to the humble,"** and yet also that **"God**

resisteth (sets Himself against) the proud." This is an indispensable truth to be lived out by every person who is to be with Jesus in the New Jerusalem.

Before we think to go any further in our lives, we should consider that there will be no blessed grace from Heaven outside of our offering true humility before the LORD. God told us that He sets Himself against (**"resisteth"**) those who have a heart of pride (**"the proud"**). There is no divine life or spiritual progress to be made in the heart of the prideful, especially if he chooses to cover his sins instead of repenting of them and relinquishing them.

> **"He that covereth his sins shall not prosper: but whoso confesseth and forsaketh them shall have mercy." Proverbs 28:13**

> The proud of heart are an abomination to the LORD (detestable in His holy eyes) and under His holy wrath, regardless of whether or not they believe they are saved, or what their past experience with the LORD might have been (Ezek. 33:12-13).

The Peril of Pride

> **"These six things doth the LORD hate: yea, seven are an abomination unto him: <u>A proud look</u>, a lying tongue, and hands that shed innocent blood ..." Proverbs 6:16-17**

The **"abomination"** listed here in the LORD's top 7 list, deals with the sinful pride of man's heart that would cause him to look down upon others instead of condescending to men of low estate – **"a proud look."** Those whose hearts are unduly filled with self-love and self-esteem, fruits of sinful pride, arrogantly look down upon others from their self-elevated positions. Their positions of self-importance exists only in their own minds and not in reality, and certainly not in the mind of Him who is

Judge and Ultimate Determiner of all. This will be borne out in the near future, as the LORD Almighty reduces all who have elevated themselves to shambles and shame, and lifts up to reign with Him all who have chosen to fear and honor Him by bowing down before His Majestic glory in the utter flatness of humility.

> **"A man's pride shall bring him low: but honour shall uphold the humble in spirit." Proverbs 19:23**

> **"Before destruction the heart of man is haughty, and before honour is humility." Proverbs 18:12**

> **"Pride goeth before destruction, and an haughty spirit before a fall." Proverbs 16:18**

When God's love fills the true Christian, love divine abounds in his life, and this love **"vaunteth not itself, is not puffed up."** (1 Cor. 13:4) The true disciple of Christ loves everyone with God's love. He is broken, humbled, and dead to self, and therefore a vessel filled with the One who **"is love."** (1 Jn. 4:7-8, 16). The measure of our Christianity is seen in how we serve others or ourselves. The fruit of the presence and work of the LORD in us can be witnessed in how well we serve others.

> **"<u>Mind not high things, but condescend to men of low estate</u>. Be not wise in your own conceits." Romans 12:16**

Get down! Take cover in humility – under the shadow of His holy wing.

Mind if I speak with candor? If for *any* reason, you believe that you are better than someone else, you are in the gall of iniquity and must repent if you are going to experience relationship with Christ, both here and eternally. Hell awaits all who live and die in pride, refusing to repent before a God and Judge who told us He is holy, and holds no tolerance for the sin of pride.

Let's gain some perspective from the Almighty.

> **"For thus saith the high and lofty One that inhabiteth eternity, whose name is Holy; I dwell in the high and holy place, with him also that is of a contrite and humble spirit, to revive the spirit of the humble, and to revive the heart of the contrite ones." Isaiah 57:15**

If God, who inhabits eternity and **"whose name is Holy,"** personally came down to this sin-cursed world to be the Cure for our root dilemma, how in His creation could I possibly not be flattened in humility at His **"unspeakable gift"**?! (2 Cor. 9:15) If He who is infinite and Almighty, the very Creator and King of Heaven and earth, lovingly condescends to us – **"men of low estate"** – how unfathomable it is for us to ever look down on any other person (in heart attitude). Such an iniquitous disposition is an **"abomination"** – it's **"A proud look."** **"A proud look"** is a look coming from a wicked heart that does not understand some basic truth about how depraved and in need of God's mercy we all are (Jer. 17:9).

Those who are humbled before God possess the fruit of humility and love all people. They love their neighbor as their own selves and prefer others above themselves (Matt. 7:12; 22:37-40; Phil. 2:3-5). The humble servant is the only true servant of Christ's eternal kingdom. He is unbiased and **"without partiality,"** which is **"hypocrisy."** (James 3:17)

> **"But if ye have bitter envying and strife in your**

> **hearts, glory not, and lie not against the truth. This wisdom descendeth not from above, but is earthly, sensual, devilish. For where envying and strife is, there is confusion and every evil work. But the wisdom that is from above is first pure, then peaceable, gentle, and easy to be intreated, full of mercy and good fruits, without partiality, and without hypocrisy." James 3:14-17**

Jesus made it clear that initial and ongoing humility is essential to entering His kingdom.

> **"And said, Verily I say unto you, Except ye be converted, and become as little children, ye shall not enter into the kingdom of heaven. Whosoever therefore shall humble himself as this little child, the same is greatest in the kingdom of heaven." Matthew 18:3-4**

Those who humble themselves to serve the LORD and His beloved people will receive the greatest everlasting rewards in the coming kingdom.

> **"But he that is greatest among you shall be your servant. And whosoever shall exalt himself shall be abased; and he that shall humble himself shall be exalted." Matthew 23:11-12**

If we exalt ourselves (being lifted up in pride), we shall be humbled downward (ultimately, if there is not full repentance). Yet if we humble ourselves (die downward), He will exalt us upward for His present and eternal glory.

The very next words out of our LORD's mouth (in Matthew 23) make it clear that the pride of those claiming to know Him actually shuts men, who would otherwise enter, out of His kingdom!

> "But woe unto you, scribes and Pharisees, hypocrites! for ye shut up the kingdom of heaven against men: for ye neither go in yourselves, neither suffer ye them that are entering to go in." Matthew 23:13

Jesus told these religionists that their pride was preventing and would continue to prevent them from **"entering"** His kingdom. In the big picture of things, pride is going to be short lived. Christ also told these religionists that **"ye are of your father the devil."** (Jn. 8:44) He then says that Satan **"abode (remained) not in the truth."** (Jn. 8:44)

In Matthew 18:3, the Son of God gave us 2 prerequisites for entering His Father's eternal kingdom:

1. One must be converted.
2. One must become as a little child – humble and dependent upon the LORD.

Those who choose sinful and self-serving pride will be humbled to hell with their master, who is the **"king over all the children of pride."** (Job 41:34) Our lives on earth are brief and yet hold eternal consequences.

> "The triumphing of the wicked is short, and the joy of the hypocrite but for a moment?" Job 20:5

Humility is the ironclad evidence of every true follower of Jesus, and a non-negotiable essential for any person who will enter the LORD's eternal kingdom. Untold blessings lie ahead for all those who choose to live humbly before their Maker.

> "By humility and the fear of the LORD are riches, and honour, and life." Proverbs 22:4

"Riches, and honour, and life" are the blessings that follow **"humility and the fear of the LORD."** God richly honors those who fear Him and are therefore humbled before Him. He raises up all those who refuse to raise up themselves. He lifts, blesses, and uses them for His good and glory (Matt. 23:12; James 4:10). Blessed resurrection life is the upward result of the life planted downward, and this is the place from which ministry springs. Look at what the apostle Paul wrote in this regard:

> **"Always bearing about in the body the dying of the Lord Jesus, that the life also of Jesus might be made manifest in our body. For we which live are always delivered unto death for Jesus' sake, that the life also of Jesus might be made manifest in our mortal flesh. So then death worketh in us, but life in you." 2 Corinthians 4:10-12**

Jesus declared to us that He came to make captives free from sin and Satan – **"If the Son therefore shall make you free, ye shall be free indeed."** (Lk. 4:18; Jn. 8:31-32, 36). There is chain-shattering, freeing power (liberty) in the redeeming blood of Christ and by the power of the Holy Ghost (Lk. 4:18; Jn. 8:36; Acts 26:18; Col. 1:12-14; 1 Pet. 1:18-19; Rev. 12:11). The divine promise is that when one bows down before the LORD, every yoke shall be broken by Him who is above all (Isa. 58). No stronghold or bond of Satan has power when Christ's blood is applied in sincere repentance and by the power of the Holy Ghost! The saint who is raised up after being bowed down, will glorify God in rich fruitfulness, being **"changed into the same image (Christ's) from glory to glory, *even* as by the Spirit of the Lord."**

> **"Now the Lord is that Spirit: and where the Spirit of the Lord *is*, there is liberty. But we all, with open face beholding as in a glass the glory**

> **of the Lord, are changed into the same image from glory to glory, *even* as by the Spirit of the Lord." 2 Corinthians 3:17-18**

It is the divine Person of the Holy Ghost who raised up the LORD, who was bowed down before His Father in death in order to purchase His Church with His own sinless blood (Acts 20:28). In like manner, it is the Holy Spirit with His resurrection power who raises up those who are bowed down before His throne of grace.

> **"And he (Jesus) was teaching in one of the synagogues on the sabbath. And, behold, there was a woman which had a spirit of infirmity eighteen years, and was bowed together, and could in no wise lift up *herself*. And when Jesus saw her, he called her to him, and said unto her, Woman, thou art loosed from thine infirmity. And he laid his hands on her: and immediately she was made straight, and glorified God... And ought not this woman, being a daughter of Abraham, whom Satan hath bound, lo, these eighteen years, be loosed from this bond on the sabbath day? And when he had said these things, all his adversaries were ashamed: and all the people rejoiced for all the glorious things that were done by him." Luke 13:10-13, 16-17**

There can be no resurrection until there is first a death. That's what baptism represents or symbolizes – you go under (death) and then are raised up in and by His resurrection power to live a new life, a life sanctified in and to Christ.

Let's look at a passage from Romans 6. Watch for the Gospel in this passage, okay – the death, burial, and resurrection:

> **"Know ye not, that so many of us as were baptized into Jesus Christ were baptized into his death? Therefore we are buried with him by baptism into death: that like as Christ was raised up from the dead by the glory of the Father, even so we also should walk in newness of life. For if we have been planted together in the likeness of his death, we shall be also in the likeness of his resurrection: Knowing this, that our old man is crucified with him, that the body of sin might be destroyed, that henceforth we should not serve sin. For he that is dead is freed from sin. Now if we be dead with Christ, we believe that we shall also live with him: Knowing that Christ being raised from the dead dieth no more; death hath no more dominion over him. For in that he died, he died unto sin once: but in that he liveth, he liveth unto God. Likewise reckon ye also yourselves to be dead indeed unto sin, but alive unto God through Jesus Christ our Lord." Romans 6:3-11**

Positionally, you are dead, buried, and raised up. You are raised up from your previously dead state, which resulted from having been born in sin. Now the life of God is in you – He who raised Jesus from the dead has now raised you up to **"newness of life."** (Rom. 6:4; 8:11)

Death to the old man – who was living according to the sinful dictates – happens *positionally* when He finds and saves us. Water baptism is a symbol of such a death, burial, and resurrection. The LORD of life saves, then buries us **"with him,"** that He might raise us up in His holy power (Rom. 6:4). This is first an inner death and begins to transform the outer life. Perhaps the LORD orchestrates external circumstances and things to further cause the saint to have to die – to sink down into the death of Christ, to be overwhelmed or covered over by death, a death out of which only God can raise us. We are not alone – as He often promised, He is ever with His saints to bring about and raise up the victory only He can manifest. This victory will ultimately culminate in our being raised up to Heaven with Him. Study 1 Corinthians 15:51-57.

The LORD bless each of us to be possessed with the revelation of our need to sink down deep into His death and burial, that He might raise us up in His glory!

Water baptism merely symbolizes the work of Christ through His Gospel in us – the death, burial, and resurrection. When we submit by His grace to being **"buried with him,"** we are then **"risen with *him* through the faith of the operation of God, who hath raised him from the dead."** (Rom. 6:4; Col. 2:12)

He is not going to abandon His own. When we submit to His non-negotiable process, He then raises us up in new life – His glorious life. – **"he hath said, I will never leave thee, nor forsake thee."** (Heb. 13:5)

Concerning baptism, Travis Bryan III writes:

> "The first definition of the word 'baptism' is *to be immersed or submerged in afflictions and difficulties to the point where one is completely overwhelmed.* This gives us the concrete meaning of the abstract statement 'dying to self.' It means 'to hit bottom' or 'reach your wits end,' where you no longer trust in self and 'put no confidence in the flesh.'"

A seed is dead or dormant then planted and germinates,

bringing forth bud, then a stalk and ultimately fruit – but first it must be buried *downward* in order to spring forth and bear life-giving fruit *upward* (Mk. 4:28). The life buried with Christ will be lifted up by His divine power and bear much fruit to God's glory (Jn. 12:24-26; 15:1-16).

> **"But if the Spirit of him that raised UP Jesus from the dead dwell in you, he that raised UP Christ from the dead shall also quicken (make alive upward) your mortal bodies by his Spirit that dwelleth in you." Romans 8:11**

Our LORD had to first die and be buried **"downward"** in order to be raised **"upward"** by the Father in resurrection life, to raise up and justify all those who would call upon Him in repentance (Rom. 1:4; 8:11; 10:13). In order for fruit to be borne **"upward,"** the disciple must first be planted **"downward"** in **"the fellowship of his sufferings, being made conformable unto his death."** (Isa. 37:31; Phil. 3:10)

> **"Buried with him in baptism, wherein also ye are risen with *him* through the faith of the operation of God, who hath raised him from the dead." Colossians 2:12**

Note that in Christ we are **"buried"** and **"risen."** It's only as we remain **"buried"** in Him that we are also **"risen"** with Him.

Man is created with the ability to **"choose."** (Josh. 24:15) Jesus told us that in the end there will be **"the resurrection of life"** and also **"the resurrection of damnation."** (Jn. 5:28-29) Each of us will be in one of these resurrections – either everlasting *life* or eternal *death* (conscious separation from God in hell). God did His part by sending His only begotten Son (Jn. 3:16). The entrance into Heaven or termination into hell will hinge upon whom we served – God or self (Rom. 6:16).

"Raised Up" into Ministry

> **"Knowing that he which raised up the Lord Jesus shall raise up us also by Jesus, and shall present us with you." 2 Corinthians 4:14**

Ministry should be an everyday occurrence in the life of the saint. There should be an overflow of God's grace in our lives that spills onto and affects those around us. The Psalmist said **"thou anointest my head with oil; my cup runneth over."** (Ps. 23:5)

Blessed **"promotion"** into heavenly glory comes only from the Giver and Sustainer of all life. He is upward, in the north (Heaven).

> **"For promotion *cometh* neither from the east, nor from the west, nor from the south. But God *is* the judge: he putteth down one, and setteth up another." Psalms 75:6-7**

That person who freely chooses to believe God, taking Christ at His Word, bowing humbly under His infinite glory, will be **"raised up"** both now and forever and eternally glorified with the Alpha and Omega (Rom. 8:11; Phil. 2:5-11; 2 Thess. 2:13-14).

Many today seek temporal glory and crowns and will be utterly shocked and abased in the next world, as they find themselves without the only redemptive Treasure (Jesus) that would have otherwise admitted them into heavenly splendor (Prov. 16:18; Matt. 6:19-21; 7:19-23; 21:44; 23:12; Jn. 5:29; 1 Cor. 9:24-27).

The Savior's Shine on the Servant

Those who love and adore and worship Him wear His presence on their countenance. It cannot be hidden. Jesus told us to **"Let your light so shine before men, that they may see your good works, and glorify your Father which is in heaven."** (Matt. 5:16)

Those whom the LORD shines upon will also shine. His resurrection life raises up those who are bowed down in utter humility before Him. The light of His shining countenance upon them will be reflected in the lives of those that behold His holy face (2 Cor. 3:18).

> **"And the LORD spake unto Moses, saying, Speak unto Aaron and unto his sons, saying, On this wise ye shall bless the children of Israel, saying unto them, The LORD bless thee, and keep thee: The LORD make his face shine upon thee, and be gracious unto thee: The LORD lift up his countenance upon thee, and give thee peace." Numbers 6:24-26**

> **"Why art thou cast down, O my soul? and why art thou disquieted in me? hope thou in God: for I shall yet praise him for the help of his countenance … hope thou in God: for I shall yet praise him, <u>who is the health of my countenance, and my God</u>." Psalms 42:5, 11**

The following verses depict salvation and a portion of its effect in the life of the recipient of His salvation:

> **"For they got not the land in possession by their own sword, neither did their own arm save them: but thy right hand, and thine arm, and the light of thy countenance, because thou hadst a favour unto them." Psalms 44:3**

"Blessed is the people that know the joyful sound: they shall walk, O LORD, in the light of thy countenance." Psalms 89:15

"A merry heart maketh a cheerful countenance: but by sorrow of the heart the spirit is broken." Proverbs 15:13

"Thou hast made known to me the ways of life; thou shalt make me full of joy with thy countenance." Acts 2:28

"And such trust have we through Christ to Godward: Not that we are sufficient of ourselves to think any thing as of ourselves; but our sufficiency is of God; Who also hath made us able ministers of the new testament; not of the letter, but of the spirit: for the letter killeth, but the spirit giveth life. But if the ministration of death, written and engraven in stones, was glorious, so that the children of Israel could not stedfastly behold the face of Moses for the glory of his countenance; which glory was to be done away: How shall not the ministration of the spirit be rather glorious? For if the ministration of condemnation be glory, much more doth the ministration of righteousness exceed in glory. For even that which was made glorious had no glory in this respect, by reason of the glory that excelleth. For if that which is done away was glorious, much more that which remaineth is glorious. Seeing then that we have such hope, we use great plainness of speech: And not as Moses, which put a vail over his face, that the children of Israel could not stedfastly look to the end of that which is abolished ... And not as Moses, which put a vail over his face, that the children of Israel could not sted-

> **fastly look to the end of that which is abolished: But we all, with open face beholding as in a glass the glory of the Lord, are changed into the same image from glory to glory, even as by the Spirit of the Lord." 2 Corinthians 3:4-13, 17-18**

When the light of Christ shines within and then through His child, it pierces into the darkness of men's hearts, men who at first may shun the light of His truth, and later turn and run to Him in repentance and faith.

> **"And the servant of the Lord must not strive; but be gentle unto all *men*, apt to teach, patient, In meekness instructing those that oppose themselves; if God peradventure will give them repentance to the acknowledging of the truth; And *that* they may recover themselves out of the snare of the devil, who are taken captive by him at his will." 2 Timothy 2:24-26**

It takes the cross – to go down flattened before Him in worship – to temper the saint in all aspects of the Christ-glorifying life. **"Temperance"** is one of the nine fruits of the Holy Spirit produced in the crucified and abiding disciple (Jn. 15; Gal. 5:22-23). **"Joy"** and **"peace"** are also of the nine.

> "We must let him who is within us shine forth, so men must admit that it could be nothing but God's transforming grace that empowers us to live with such charity and goodness.
>
> You ask what is the good of being good. Your oppressors vaunt themselves over you, take every advantage of your gentleness, and misinterpret your self-restraint. But it may be that your kindness is beginning to thaw the frozen soil in another's heart. The warmth emitted by your benevolence

may, at first, seem to make no difference, but every hour of sunshine melts ice-covered souls a little bit more. Show kindness to all men, and trust God with the results." F.B. Meyer, *The Best of F.B. Meyer,* p. 166

Jesus instructed us to **"Let your light so shine before men"** so that they will **"see your good works and glorify your Father which is in heaven."** (Matt. 5:16)

Those who are planted deeply into Christ will flourish and be fruitful.

> **"The righteous shall flourish like the palm tree: he shall grow like a cedar in Lebanon. Those that be planted in the house of the LORD shall flourish in the courts of our God. They shall still bring forth fruit in old age; they shall be fat and flourishing." Psalms 92:12-14**

PRAYER: *Jesus, thank You for dying for my sins to ransom my soul from certain damnation. Thank You, heavenly Father, for the propitiatory death of Jesus Christ, and for raising up Your only begotten Son to justify and empower Your people by Your Spirit to please You in all things in this brief life on earth. Thank You for Your body, Jesus. I am dead to self, sin, and this world and buried with Thee. Thank You for raising me up to new life – for You are the resurrection and the life. It is no longer I that live but rather Christ! Bless this life You granted to be more deeply grounded in Christ – to sink down into His death – and to love, serve, and become more fruitful for Your eternal glory. Let Your blessed heavenly glory shine in and on and through my life. Amen.*

Capture Points

- Discuss Colossians 2:11-12, and remember this passage is not referring to water baptism.

- On index cards, transcribe Proverbs 16:18 and 22:4.

- Discuss according to the fullness of Holy Scripture (Isa. 28:10, 13; 1 Cor. 2:13; 2 Cor. 13:1).

- Openly talk about **"promotion"** and what it entails in the divine economy.

- Begin at Psalms 75:6-7, and also look at Matthew 20:24-28 and 1 Corinthians 9:24-27.

Chapter Nine

"The Gospel which I Preached unto You"
1 Corinthians 15:1

> "Moreover, brethren, I declare unto you the gospel which I preached unto you, which also ye have received, and wherein ye stand; By which also ye are saved, if ye keep in memory what I preached unto you, unless ye have believed in vain. For I delivered unto you first of all that which I also received, how that Christ died for our sins according to the scriptures; And that he was buried, and that he rose again the third day according to the scriptures." 1 Corinthians 15:1-4

Here we are instructed to **"keep in memory"** the gospel of Christ that Paul preached, or we will have **"believed in vain."** What he shows us here is the true **"gospel"** –

"... Christ died for our sins according to the scriptures; and that he (Jesus) was buried, and that he rose again the third day according to the scriptures." (1 Cor. 15:1-4)

So according to 1 Corinthians 15:1-4, the Gospel is defined as:

> **" ... Christ died for our sins"**
>
> **"he (Jesus) was buried"**
>
> **"he rose again the third day"**

Could Jesus have been buried or raised again before He first died? No.

> **"Thou fool, that which thou sowest is not quickened, except it die." 1 Corinthians 15:36**

Are we keeping the cross – the centrality of the Gospel of Jesus – in mind? Jesus not only died on a cross to bring us to God, He commanded that all who would follow Him take up their cross. His true disciples are to glory in the cross – the death of self giving rise to the resurrection life of the LORD.

Paul the apostle forcefully affirmed:

> **"But God forbid that I should glory, save in the cross of our Lord Jesus Christ, by whom the world is crucified unto me, and I unto the world." Galatians 6:14**

Concerning the preaching of Christ and the cross, Charles Spurgeon said:

> "I believe that those sermons which are fullest of Christ are the most likely to be blessed to the conversion of the hearers. Let your sermons be full of Christ, from beginning to end crammed full of the

gospel. As for myself, brethren, I cannot preach anything else but Christ and His cross, for I know nothing else, and long ago, like the apostle Paul, I determined not to know anything else save Jesus Christ and Him crucified. People have often asked me, 'What is the secret of your success?' I always answer that I have no other secret but this, that I have preached the gospel,—not about the gospel, but the gospel,—the full, free, glorious gospel of the living Christ who is the incarnation of the good news."

Is the Modern Church Self-centered or Christ-centered?

Scarcely can one find the message of the cross being preached today. What a shame! This was Paul's Gospel and if it is not ours, we have a false gospel, **"another gospel,"** and in His holy eyes are **"accursed"** for espousing a cross-less gospel (Gal. 1:6-9). How can Christ possibly be glorified where His message is shunned, and men are therefore alive unto self and dead to Him instead of dead to self and alive to Him? How can the Gospel – death, burial, and resurrection – be seen if men aren't learning to die, being buried with Him, and allowing Him to raise them up in His life and power? How can personality, programs, and pitiful political and philosophical panderings possibly replace Him who is **"Alpha and Omega, the beginning and the ending, saith the Lord, which is, and which was, and which is to come, the Almighty."** (Rev. 1:8)

Glory-Robbing & Soul-Stealing

The brazenly rebellious refusal of any leader to die to self and preach Christ crucified, is the betrayal of Christ and precious eternal souls.

> **"And on this manner did Absalom to all Israel that came to the king for judgment: so <u>Absalom stole the hearts of the men of Israel</u>." 2 Samuel 15:6**

Self-centered or Christ-centered? Like Absalom, who **"stole the hearts of the men of Israel,"** so many mislead those they guide into darkness, deception, and ultimately damnation. Most men in positions of "Christian" leadership and influence do not elevate Jesus Christ, the one and only **"Head"** of His true Church (Eph. 5:23; Col. 1:18; 2:18-19). Instead, they elevate themselves, the programs of mere men, pageantry, entertainment, and the doctrine of self-love.

> **"For we are the circumcision, which worship God in the spirit, and rejoice in Christ Jesus, and have no confidence in the flesh." Philippians 3:3**

It is sad that so many leaders today have an Absalom spirit. They work the same evil he did – stealing the heart affections away from the King who alone deserves the glory. Judgment is coming and no flesh is going to glory in His holy presence (1 Cor. 1:29, 31; 1 Pet. 4:17-18).

> **"… Absalom stole the hearts of the men of Israel." 2 Samuel 15:6**

Any "Christian" leader who is not regularly preaching Christ's cross and how it applies in propitiation and the personal application of dying to self, is utterly false. A cross-less gospel is a false gospel.

> "How these churches would grow (spiritually) if pastors would give up control and allow themselves to be crucified. 'Thou fool, that which thou sowest is not quickened unless it dies.' (1 Cor.

15:36) He would raise their congregations (environment) from the dead. The only place intimacy with Christ and revival can be found is in His wounds." Travis Bryan III

When we are crucified and sunk down into Christ's death, He who is **"the resurrection and the life,"** and also the Holy Ghost who raised Christ from the dead, will reign in us to magnify Himself! (Jn. 11:25; Rom. 8:11) How can men be quickened and moved from self-indulgence to the crucified life if in fact they rarely or never hear the biblical message of the cross? How can the message of the true Gospel be forged in their hearts with deep conviction, when they are being led to serve self through counterfeit leaders who are self-serving wolves who wear sheep's clothing? (Isa. 56:10-12; Matt. 7:15; Phil. 3:18-19)

"And that he died for all, that they which live should not henceforth live unto themselves, but unto him which died for them, and rose again." 2 Corinthians 5:15

A. W. Tozer, in an apt description of the contemporary church, warned that:

"Shallow leadership would modify the cross to please the entertainment-mad saintlings who will have their fun even within the very sanctuary. But to engage in such a modification of the gospel is to court spiritual disaster." The LORD is calling for men who will choose the fear of the LORD and live their lives in the Spirit (Prov. 1:29; Rom. 8:14; Gal. 5:16). This is the crucified life and those who are living it preach it – those who don't, can't and won't. Christ and the cross were the center point of Paul's message (1 Cor. 2:2; Gal. 2:20; 6:14). Any man not willing to live and preach the cross is a ravenous/devouring wolf and will lead others into the same darkness he himself relishes (Jer. 13:16; Jn. 3:19-21; 2 Thess. 2:10-12).

Make no mistake: According to Jesus, a cross-less gospel is of satanic origin and all who do not sufficiently preach the cross are also of Satan. What has one profited if he has not lost his life in order to be apprehended and swallowed up of Christ's life?

> **"But he turned, and said unto Peter, Get thee behind me, Satan: thou art an offence unto me: for thou savourest not the things that be of God, but those that be of men. Then said Jesus unto his disciples, If ANY man will come after me, let him deny himself, and take up his cross, and follow me. For whosoever will save his life shall lose it: and whosoever will lose his life for my sake shall find it. For what is a man profited, if he shall gain the whole world, and lose his own soul? or what shall a man give in exchange for his soul?" Matthew 16:23-26**

The Greek word for **"deny"** here is *aparneomai* and means *to deny utterly, disown.*

We as His purchased possession have been apprehended of God, bought by His own blood, and saved into His eternal family.

> **"Ye also, as lively stones, are built up a spiritual house, an holy priesthood, to offer up spiritual sacrifices, acceptable to God by Jesus Christ ... But ye are a chosen generation, a royal priesthood, an holy nation, a peculiar people; that ye should shew forth the praises of him who hath called you out of darkness into his marvellous light: Which in time past were not a people, but are now the people of God: which had not obtained mercy, but now have obtained**

mercy. Dearly beloved, I beseech you as strangers and pilgrims, abstain from fleshly lusts, which war against the soul." 1 Peter 2:5, 9-11

Being His very own **"royal priesthood,"** we give up all rights to ourselves and yield our lives, to be entirely led of Him who alone is worthy (2 Cor. 5:15). Like Christ, we utterly disown and deny our own will that His will might be done in us (Lk. 22:42).

Concerning Matthew 16:24-28, William MacDonald writes in the *Believer's Bible Commentary* (emphasis his):

"Preparation for True Discipleship (16:24-28)

> **16:24** Now the Lord Jesus plainly states what is involved in being His disciple: denial of self, cross-bearing, and following Him. To **deny** self is not the same as self-denial; it means to yield to His control so completely that self has no rights whatever. To **take up** the **cross** means the willingness to endure shame, suffering, and perhaps martyrdom for His sake; to die to sin, self, and the world. To follow Him means to live as He lived with all that involves of humility, poverty, compassion, love, grace, and every other godly virtue.
>
> **16:25** The Lord anticipates two hindrances to discipleship. The first is the natural temptation **to save** oneself from discomfort, pain, loneliness, or loss. The other is to become wealthy. As to the first, Jesus warned that those who hug their lives for selfish purposes would never find fulfillment; those who recklessly abandon their lives to Him, not counting the cost, would find the reason for their existence.
>
> **16:26** The second temptation – that of getting rich – is irrational. 'Suppose,' said Jesus, 'that **a man**

became so successful in business that he owned **the whole world**. This mad quest would absorb so much of his time and energy that he would miss the central purpose of his life. What good would it do to make all that money, then die, leave it all behind, and spend eternity empty-handed?' Man is here for bigger business than to make money. He is called to represent the interests of his King. If he misses that, he misses everything.

In verse 24, Jesus told them the worst. That is characteristic of Christianity; you know the worst at the outset. But you never cease discovering the treasures and the blessings. Barnhouse put it well:

> 'When one has seen all that is forbidding in the Scriptures, there is not left hidden that can come as a surprise, every new thing which we shall ever learn in this life or the next will come as a delight.'" pp. 1268, 1269

As one is taken by Christ into the burial of the self-life, he will steadily lose his grip on and affection for the momentary trinkets of this passing world, and for the glamour and praise of mere men. Moved by the fear of the LORD, his allegiance and the affections of his heart will then begin to ascend to the **"glorious high throne from the beginning"** which **"is the place of our sanctuary."** (Jer. 17:12)

> **"While we look not at the things which are seen, but at the things which are not seen: for the things which are seen are temporal; but the things which are not seen are eternal." 2 Corinthians 4:18**

What are we clinching and clinging to in this life? What shall our temporal glory do for us in that Day? What are we not willing to lay down for the love of God? (Jude 21) What might we be counting and esteeming to be greater in importance than Jesus? What idol of heart might remain in us? (Ezek. 14:3) What are our lives saying to others who see the dissimulation and inconsistencies of our own personal walks? (2 Cor. 6:3-4) What shall we say to Him whose glory we stole away from those souls which we led astray from Him? (2 Sam. 15:6; Matt. 12:30) What shall be our end? What shall we say to Him who bled to save those we steered away from Him?

"The Pillar and Ground of the Truth"

> **"But if I tarry long, that thou mayest know how thou oughtest to behave thyself in the house of God, which is the church of the living God, the pillar and ground of the truth. And without controversy great is the mystery of godliness: God was manifest in the flesh, justified in the Spirit, seen of angels, preached unto the Gentiles, believed on in the world, received up into glory." 1 Timothy 3:15-16**

Just as Christ was born in or **"manifest in the flesh"** and **"justified in the Spirit"** and then **"received up into glory,"** so is the life of the true saint. He is first **"born of flesh,"** then **"born (justified) of the Spirit,"** and will ultimately be raised up to Heaven to be in the glory of God (Jn. 3:1-8).

According to 1 Timothy 3:15-16, the **"church of the living God"** is the **"pillar and ground of the truth"** and should be ever preaching the true Gospel, which is the death, burial, and resurrection of Jesus and His saints both now and eternally. This is most certainly the true Word of the original Gospel which Paul charged Timothy to **"preach,"** knowing that the hour was coming when men would turn from hearing the truth and would be turned to a false gospel of ease and self-gratification.

> "I charge thee therefore before God, and the Lord Jesus Christ, who shall judge the quick and the dead at his appearing and his kingdom; Preach the word; be instant in season, out of season; reprove, rebuke, exhort with all longsuffering and doctrine. For the time will come when they will not endure sound doctrine; but after their own lusts shall they heap to themselves teachers, having itching ears; And they shall turn away their ears from the truth, and shall be turned unto fables." 2 Timothy 4:1-4

Any gospel that does not regularly include the cross is a fable, and those preaching such are false teachers.

Predestined to be Conformed to His Image

Christ's saints are not just predestined to have their sins washed away, they are predestined to be conformed to His image which is death, burial, and resurrection. Many today want their sins washed away and a ticket to Heaven, but refuse or never hear the message of the cross. This is tragic!

> "Thou fool, that which thou sowest is not quickened (made alive), except it die." 1 Corinthians 15:36

Note the key words in the above verse – **"quickened"** and **"die."** We are fools to believe that God is going to quicken (raise up) the person who will not first **"die."** Just as the seed cannot begin to germinate and bring forth a crop and fruit until it first die downward into the ground, even so, God will not germinate and bring forth the fruit of His life in us until we freely go downward in humility and death to self.

Colossians 1:20 says:

> **"And, having made peace through the blood of his cross (death), by him to reconcile (resurrection) all things unto himself; by him, I say, whether they be things in earth, or things in heaven." Colossians 1:20**

Reconciling all things to Himself requires the Gospel – death, burial, and resurrection or raising up (1 Cor. 15:1-4). All those who have been brought by Him into His kingdom **"he also did predestinate to be conformed to the image of his Son ..."** (Rom. 8:29) He therefore purposely orchestrates all things in our lives to conform us to Christ's crucified and raised up image. He never said that in this life all things would be just or fair or good, but rather that He works all things together **"for good to them that love God."** (Rom. 8:28) When we love God supremely as He commanded, we will willingly allow Him to conform us to the image of His Son by death, burial, and resurrection. Our heavenly Father is the Master Orchestrator of all things and will be glorified in His true remnant saints **"in whom is all"** His **"delight."** (Ps. 16:3)

> **"And we know that all things work together for good to them that love God, to them who are the called according to his purpose. For whom he did foreknow, he also did predestinate to be conformed to the image of his Son, that he might be the firstborn among many brethren." Romans 8:28-29**

As Christ died on the cross for the sins of the world, so those apprehended by Him are to die the death of their flesh life and love for the world. Jesus Christ is the true Gospel, and those called and justified by Him are predestined to be conformed to His image, in the likeness of His death, burial, and resurrection.

> **"Moreover whom he did predestinate, them he also called: and whom he called, them he also**

justified: and whom he justified, them he also glorified." Romans 8:30

"All men" He did **"predestinate"** to be saved, and yet only some will answer that call (1 Tim. 2:4; 2 Pet. 3:9). Those who answer His call affirmatively are the **"called"** and are by Him **"justified"** and **"glorified,"** which is something that is presently true and also will be manifest when we meet Him.

The Order of the Gospel

There are many who will readily preach the predestination of this passage and yet not the conformity to Christ's image. They personally walk and teach the road of ease, and this is clear in that they attach no personal responsibility to the called individual to yield to the Spirit in crucifixion of the self-life (Rom. 8:13). These are those **"ungodly men"** who are **"turning the grace of our God into lasciviousness (license for sin), and denying the only Lord God, and our Lord Jesus Christ."** (Jude 3-4)

By doing such, these leaders betray the One who bled on the cross and commanded all who will come after Him to deny self and take up their cross as they follow Him (Lk. 9:23-24). These false leaders call men to worship at the altar of self. They beckon them to try to experience their best lives now, reinvent themselves, or esteem themselves in this sinful world instead of pointing them to the resurrection glorification that is coming to all those who willingly and obediently suffer the death of self. The LORD simply will not glorify or resurrect and grant eternal victory to any person who tries to circumvent His way – the cross.

> **"Verily, verily, I say unto you, Except a corn (grain) of wheat fall into the ground and die, it abideth alone: but if it die, it bringeth forth**

much fruit." John 12:24

Those who love self so much and therefore will not fall down flat and die, will abide alone for eternity – apart from God – in **"outer darkness."** (Matt. 8:12)

What is the order of the Gospel?

Death

Burial

Resurrection

This order cannot be altered. It is fixed or ironclad. The Gospel is first the death, then the burial, and only then the resurrection of Jesus. The LORD will not change (Mal. 3:6) This is the divine and non-negotiable order. By teaching a supposed victory before or without a preceding death and burial, smiling, modern-day beguilers teach a false gospel. These are the prophesied false prophets who are leading **"many"** to eternal damnation (Matt. 7:15; 24:3-5; 11, 24; 1 Tim. 4:1-3; 2 Tim. 3:13; 2 Pet. 2:1-3).

Was not Christ's victory or raising up preceded by His first dying and being buried? In God's economy, there can be no victory without a foregoing and willing death to self – the burial of the old man with his sinful deeds. The **"sting of death"** can possess no power over that one who is dead and buried with Christ (1 Cor. 15:56).

"For he that is dead is freed from sin." Romans 6:7

Only those who are **"dead"** to self can be **"freed from sin."** The LORD will only raise up that one who is bowed down in humility before Him (Ps. 145:14; James 4:10).

Those who are conformed to His holy image are justified,

sanctified, and glorified with the Savior (Rom. 8:29-30).

When we die, giving preference to the LORD above ourselves by allowing His infinite power to completely envelope our mortal and finite frailty, then His victory is wrought, but not before we obediently lay down our lives.

> **"So when this corruptible shall have put on incorruption, and this mortal shall have put on immortality, then shall be brought to pass the saying that is written, Death is swallowed up in victory. O death, where is thy sting? O grave, where is thy victory? The sting of death is sin; and the strength of sin is the law. But thanks be to God, which giveth us the victory through our Lord Jesus Christ." 1 Corinthians 15:54-57**

Sin gives strength to death to conquer the sinner, and yet when a person dies (to self), **"Death is swallowed up in victory."** Christ's victory conquers sin when the individual saint dies to self in obedience to Jesus. At that point, the LORD's grace and Holy Spirit enable and bring forth victory (Rom. 8:13; 2 Cor. 3:18).

Just as Christ's death, burial, and resurrection wrought the victory of salvation for the whole world of men, so when we follow Him by laying down our own lives and being buried with Him, then His resurrection victory manifests in our personal lives (2 Cor. 4:10-12).

Today, so many want the rewards of Christ's victory without Christ's cross. They want the benefits His **"so great salvation"** purchased and yet without bearing His cross (Heb. 2:3, 9). This is why many migrate to teachers and churches that tickle their unrepentant ears by telling them what they *want* to hear instead of the truth they *need* to hear.

Jesus told us that **"Every one that is of the truth**

heareth my voice." (Jn. 18:37) His voice has not changed. He told us plainly that in order to follow Him, we must deny ourselves and take up the cross (Matt. 16:24-26; Lk. 9:23-24). He will raise us up in His power and life as we follow His leading and example of first laying down our own self-life.

PRAYER: *Jesus, please forge in my heart the deep desire and conviction to know You and for Your holy truth. Bless me to love Your Word and to willingly submit myself to You to be crucified with You, that You might raise me up into the victory that You alone can grant. Open my eyes to know whom the wolves are who refuse to preach Your cross and are therefore enemies of the cross of Christ. I will follow You and not mere men. In Jesus' name. Amen.*

Capture Points

- Discuss Matthew 16:23-26.
- *On an index card, write out Romans 8:29 (KJV recommended).*
- Transcribe Jeremiah 17:12 on an index card *(KJV recommended).*
- Discuss 2 Timothy 4:1-5.

SafeGuardYourSoul.com

Chapter Ten

"Death is Swallowed Up in Victory"
1 Corinthians 15:54

> "So when this corruptible shall have put on incorruption, and this mortal shall have put on immortality, then shall be brought to pass the saying that is written, Death is swallowed up in victory." 1 Corinthians 15:54

Ultimately **"death"** will be **"swallowed up in victory"** when we pass to be with Christ.

Paul said: **"Christ shall be magnified in my body, whether it be by life, or by death. For to me to live is Christ, and to die is gain."** (Phil. 1:20-21) To **"die"** (be separated from our mortal body) and go be with Christ, is **"gain."** To die to the dictates of the sinful nature is also **"gain."** Spiritual **"death"** is conquered or **"swallowed**

up" in the victory of Christ in each of these instances. Contrary to much teaching today, without our fleshly nature being **"swallowed up"** and conquered by the Spirit, and individual overcoming faith of the disciple, there will be no victory (Rom. 6:16; 1 Cor. 9:27; Rev. 3:5; 22:8, 11, 27).

> **"For we that are in *this* tabernacle (temporal body) do groan, being burdened: not for that we would be unclothed, but clothed upon, that mortality might be swallowed up of life." 2 Corinthians 5:4**

Here the Holy Ghost tells us that **"mortality"** will one day be **"swallowed up of life."** Death will be robbed of its power over those who partake with Christ, who is **"the resurrection and the life."** (Jn. 11:25) The conquering power of Christ, who is **"the life,"** is going to overtake and swallow up death like a whale swallowing a minnow (Jn. 14:6).

> **"Forasmuch then as the children are partakers of flesh and blood, he also himself likewise took part of the same; that through death he might destroy him that had the power of death, that is, the devil; And deliver them who through fear of death were all their lifetime subject to bondage." Hebrews 2:14-15**

Jesus was the only One ever qualified to pay the ultimate price to satisfy the claims of the heavenly Father's justice in redeeming His fallen creation. Christ destroyed **"him that had the power of death, that is, the devil."** As we are in Him, we need not fear because His **"perfect love (in us) casteth out all fear"** of not being with Him (Heb. 2:14-15; 1 Jn. 4:16-18).

> **"For whatsoever is born of God overcometh the world: and this is the victory that overcometh**

> **the world, even our faith. Who is he that overcometh the world, but he that believeth that Jesus is the Son of God?" 1 John 5:4-5**

In order to partake of Christ in eternity, one must be willing to first partake of Him in this life – according to the way He prescribed to us in His Word (Matt. 7:21; Heb. 9:27; Rev. 22:11). He told us up-front that only a **"few"** would be willing to truly know and partake of Him in this life (Matt. 7:13-14; 21-23). It seems that the majority of people would rather deny Christ by migrating to smooth speakers who don't preach the cross and its heart-circumcising, sin-crucifying reality (1 Tim. 4:1-3; 2 Tim. 4:2-4).

> **"It is a faithful saying: For if we be dead with him, we shall also live with him: <u>IF we suffer, we shall also reign with him: IF we deny him, he also will deny us</u>." 2 Timothy 2:11-12**

Christ is denied every time one doesn't deny self. A God-fearing man once said:

> "Either Christ will crucify *self* out of the life, or *self* will crucify Christ right out of that life."

Most people today say they would rather go to Heaven than hell, and serve Christ rather than Satan. Yet regrettably, most people are not willing to **"be dead with him"** to the things of this world, and will therefore forfeit being able to eternally **"live with him."** (Rom. 6; Gal. 2:20; 5:24) They will not be blessed to forever **"reign with him"** in the life to come because they **"deny"** His lordship in this brief life (Matt. 7:21; 2 Tim. 3:5). Most people want the heavenly *crown* and yet are not willing to take up the *cross* of the heavenly King. This is the test.

Christ-glorifying victory over the sinful nature is granted when our temporary tabernacles in which we currently exist are put under subjection to the Spirit, will, and Word of God (1 Cor. 9:27). This is why Paul could say that he did **"glory in tribulations."** (Rom. 5:3)

Though found and saved by Him, we must also obey Him, and our obedience is always the proof that we possess saving faith. Though the gift of eternal life was perfectly purchased by Christ, it is not an un-forfeitable possession (Lk. 8:13; Jn. 6:66; Heb. 3:6, 12-15; 10:26-39). One who has been genuinely saved must continue or endure to the end **"through much tribulation"** to be saved (Matt. 10:22; 24:13; Acts 14:22; Col. 1:23; Heb. 3:6, 12-15). The message of the LORD and His beloved prophets and apostles was not one of ease like the messages of the wolves of our day.

Concerning Romans 16, Donald Stamps, in the *Life In the Spirit* Study Bible, writes:

> "At the end of his letter, Paul gives a strong warning to the church in Rome to be alert to all those who do damage to the church by corrupting and extorting the 'doctrine' (teaching) of Paul and the other apostles. They are to 'mark' the proponents of false doctrine and 'avoid them' and their ministry. Those marked may have been antinomians (i.e., against the law), who taught that because salvation is by grace, saving faith does not necessarily include obedience to Christ Jesus (cf. 6:1-2; 2 Cor. 4:2; 11:3; Eph. 4:14; Rev. 2:4-5). They believed that a person could live in sin and reject God's moral law, and yet possess eternal salvation. <u>These false teachers were eloquent orators, speaking with comforting words and flattering speeches (cf. Jude 16), but deceiving simple Christians.</u>" p. 1759

Those **"ungodly men"** who are in our day **"turning the grace of our God into lasciviousness (license for sin)"** through their false teachings, do great and eternal damage in their rampage to **"destroy souls."** (Isa. 9:16; Ezek. 22:25-27; Jude 3-4). We are commanded to **"earnestly contend for the faith once delivered to the saints"** against those who assume that all who have truly been saved are in no danger whatsoever of forfeiting their gift of eternal life they once received. Yet, no such assurance, language, or teaching is offered in Scripture (2 Pet. 2:20-22; 3:17; Rev. 2-3).

Ongoing personal participation is required of the individual recipient of eternal life or all will be lost (Matt. 26:41; Lk. 21:34-36; Col. 1:23; 2:8; Heb. 3:6,12-14; 10:26-39; 1 Pet. 4:17-18; 2 Pet. 2:20-22).

Salvation requires more than just the initial prayer. Jesus warned that we must **"watch and pray"** continually that we might enter His kingdom and not **"enter into temptation."** (Matt. 26:41; Lk. 21:34-36).

> "Prayer is an emptying of myself and my own lusts and desires." Andrew Murray

The life of prayer is the tangible demonstration that we are preferring Christ above self. As a result, we are granted victory over sin as His holy life teems in. As we **"watch and pray,"** our lamps or vessels are continually filled with the holy oil of His Spirit, and we are thereby kept ready to meet Him (Matt. 25:1-13; 26:41).

As His life in us is allowed to flourish through communion, **"the deeds of the body"** will be mortified and our lives will be raised up in His victory.

> **"For if ye live after the flesh, ye shall die: but if ye through the Spirit do mortify the deeds of the body, ye shall live." Romans 8:13**

In speaking with a dear brother recently, we talked

about Romans 6-8 and what the LORD has to say about the futile quest to salvage or build upon the cursed foundation of the sinful nature. The old man is "**by nature**" prone to "**disobedience.**" (Eph. 2:1-2) The sinful nature is under the power of Satan, and we – yes even His children – can become his prey if we walk in disobedience (Eph. 2:1-2). Concerning the sinful nature's propensity to be wicked when not swallowed up by Christ's consuming life, the Bible says that it is **"only evil continually."** (Gen. 6:5) Speaking of men outside of the present, relational grace of Christ, the Bible tells us that **"every imagination of the thoughts of his heart"** is **"only evil continually."** (Gen. 6:5) Note the finality of this statement on the spiritual state of men outside of Christ – **"only evil continually."** Pure evil – perpetually. This is why the rebellious nature that dwells in us must be sentenced to death (2 Cor. 1:9). Genesis 6:5 is the declaration of divine and just judgment upon those who live in the flesh and not in the Holy Spirit with the Savior. In those days, leading up to the flood of His judgment, sin was epidemic. Only 8 souls qualified to be lifted up upon the waters of salvation, riding safely in the refuge of Christ, their ark.

Those who allow the flood of God's presence and power to conquer the sins that defile them in His holy sight, will be blessed to ride the ark of His safety into eternity (Mk. 7:20; Rev. 21:27).

> **"Thou hast a few names even in Sardis which have not defiled their garments; and they shall walk with me in white: for they are worthy. He that overcometh, <u>the same shall be clothed in white raiment; and I will not blot out his name out of the book of life</u>, but I will confess his name before my Father, and before his angels." Revelation 3:4-5**

Jesus told us plainly that sin defiles or makes one unclean in the sight of God who is **"Holy, holy, holy."** (Isa. 6:3; Mk. 7:20; Heb. 12:14-15; Rev. 4:8) That person who was in the past saved, and then sinned and yet has not repented and been blessed to be forgiven, is simply unprepared to meet the LORD, no matter what his past relationship with God may have been (Ezek. 33:12-13; Rev. 21:8, 11, 27).

How did Jesus tell us that the displeasing sins of self-serving worldliness can be overcome?

> **"Watch and pray, that ye enter not into temptation: the spirit indeed is willing, but the flesh is weak." Matthew 26:41**

Andrew Murray said:

> "As I pray, let me be willing to accept my place with Him, crucified to the world, to sin, and to self."

Why did He that is **"Holy, holy, holy"** (Isa. 6:3; Rev. 4:8) judge (in His flood of Noah's day) all those who chose to live outside of Him?

> **"And GOD saw that the wickedness of man was great in the earth, and that every imagination of the thoughts of his heart was only evil continually." Genesis 6:5**

If we lack the vital understanding of the sinful nature or unalterable bent (iniquities) of our hearts outside of Christ, we won't rightly comprehend the reason for the cross of Christ and how it eternally and daily applies to us individually. With Paul, we must understand that in us, that is in our flesh, **"dwelleth no good thing."** (Rom. 7:18) It is only when swallowed up in the life of Christ that the sinful nature within is whelmed over and subdued by the power of the grace of God (Rom. 6:14; 8:1-4). It must die and be buried that He might raise us up to bring Him glory.

> **"But if the Spirit of him that raised up Jesus from the dead dwell in you, he that raised up Christ from the dead shall also quicken (resurrect; make alive) your mortal bodies by his Spirit that dwelleth in you." Romans 8:11**

By reason of the old man's nature and enmity against God, the LORD demands that it be put to death. We died and were buried *positionally* with Christ, and yet the bent of sin is said to be **"only evil continually."** (Gen. 6:5) This bent toward evil requires the ongoing task of keeping it under subjection to the power of God by regular fasting, prayer, study, and daily obedience (Rom. 6; 1 Cor. 9:27).

> **"The heart is deceitful above all things, and desperately wicked: who can know it?" Jeremiah 17:9**

Let's gain the insight revealed in the first verses of Ephesians 2:

> **"And you hath he quickened (made alive), who were dead (separated from God) in trespasses and sins; Wherein in time past ye walked according to the course of this world, according to the prince of the power of the air, the spirit that now worketh (is at work) in the children of disobedience: Among whom also we all had our conversation in times past in the lusts of our flesh, fulfilling the desires of the flesh and of the mind; and were by nature the children of wrath, even as others." Ephesians 2:1-3**

Here Paul the apostle speaks of who we *were,* and also

who we *become again,* if we live apart from vital union with Christ (Rom. 8:5-8, 13; James 1:21-25; 2 Pet. 1:9; 2:20-22).

Instead of preaching the original message of the original Gospel of Christ – that we must deny the self-life, daily putting it to death on the cross – most preaching today seeks to build upon the divinely cursed premise of the old man. *This message of the apostate church is man-centered instead of Christ-centered.* In God's economy all begins and ends with Him – **"In the beginning God created the heaven and the earth … I am Alpha and Omega, the beginning and the ending, saith the Lord, which is, and which was, and which is to come, the Almighty."** (Gen. 1:1; Rev. 1:8) The message that begins and ends with man – the created instead of the Creator – is **"another gospel"** in that it does not simply convey divine truth in its pure form – **"If they speak not according to this word, it is because there is no light in them … speak with my words unto them … preach the word … speak thou the things that become sound doctrine … if any man speak, let him speak as of the oracles of God."** (Isa. 8:20; Ezek. 3:4; 2 Tim. 4:2; Tit. 2:1; 1 Pet. 4:11) In this truth alone, most preaching today is weighed in the balance and found wanting (lacking). It is clearly a misrepresentation because men today have become so very arrogant that they are deluded into believing the notion that they are wiser than the Almighty.

> "The cross of Christ is the most revolutionary thing ever to appear … It stands high above the opinions of men and to that cross all opinions must come at last for judgment." A.W. Tozer

The God-fearing servant tends to the need so often expressed in Holy Scripture to **"daily"** deny the self-life by putting it on the cross and choosing to allow Christ's will to prevail and not his own (Lk. 9:23-24; 22:42; 2 Cor. 11:4). In doing such, the LORD Himself sustains that man in the truth – in his personal life and in ministry to others. He stands as a minority among those who hold positions of leadership.

> **"For if he that cometh preacheth <u>another Jesus</u>, whom we have not preached, or if ye receive <u>another spirit</u>, which ye have not received, or <u>another gospel</u>, which ye have not accepted, ye might well bear with him." 2 Corinthians 11:4**

The "Jesus" of the modern and apostate church world is one who has made wide provision for many to enter into eternal glory. In contrast, the one true God who reveals Himself in Holy Scripture, has informed us that the way is narrow and only a few will enter therein (Matt. 7:13-14). Beware!

The original Gospel God gave us through His prophets, only begotten Son, and apostles, includes the command to die that He might live (Jn. 12:24). He makes no exception for the slightest alteration in His message, and **"<u>any</u> other gospel"** is a false gospel.

> **"I marvel that ye are so soon removed from him that called you into the grace of Christ unto <u>another gospel</u>: Which is not another; but there be some that trouble you, and would pervert the gospel of Christ. But though we, or an angel from heaven, preach <u>any other gospel</u> unto you than that which we have preached unto you, let him be accursed." Galatians 1:6-8**

Today, man and his sinful desires are at the center of most "Christian" fad books and pulpit speech in the apostate church world. Wolves have hi-jacked the majority of positions and pulpits and penmanship in today's self-love church world. The antichrist message of their winds of false doctrine replaces the supremacy of Christ with what does best for man – to meet *his* immediate, self-serving desires apart from Christ (Col. 2:8, 19-19). To perceive this, it takes little more than reflecting upon the *best life now* type book titles (which reveal the emphasis of the book's contents) and how they are *purpose-driven* instead of Spirit-led, cross-based, and Word-driven.

In God's economy there is no salvaging the sinful nature we inherited in Adam. There is also no casting it out once and for all like we do with devils, but rather we are commanded to **"mortify the deeds of the body"** that His grace and life might abound (Rom. 6-8). He told us that the sinful nature must be daily put under. It will never reform but must be silenced by daily communion between the recipient of God's grace and the LORD, by the power of the Holy Ghost (Rom. 6:14; 8:13). The student of Christ, nourished up in His precious precepts and empowered by His Spirit and enabling grace, is given daily victory through the cross. He begins to realize from experiencing the Word that there is no solution except to daily crucify the **"deeds of the body."** (Jn. 7:17; Rom. 8:13) When we diligently begin to pursue knowing Him – the whole reason for which He created and redeemed us – we begin to gladly remove anything that hinders that blessed communion, in order that we like Paul **"may know him, and the power of his resurrection, and the fellowship of his sufferings, being made conformable unto his death."** (Phil. 3:10)

When the Holy Ghost begins to enlighten us, we will see the will of self as the enemy of Christ, and how it is at **"enmity against God: for it is not subject to the law of God, neither indeed can be."** (Rom. 8:7) He will show us how that **"they that are in the flesh cannot please God."** (Rom. 8:8) For this reason, the disciple who will know and follow Christ on that narrow path that leads to life, must **"keep under"** that sinful bent and **"bring it into subjection"** to his own and God's Spirit (Matt. 7:13-14; Lk. 9:23-24; 14:33; 1 Cor. 9:27). By this grace-enabled cooperation, we will dwell in Him who bled and be ready for His soon coming (Col. 3:1-5). Christ alone must reign supreme in the life of the remnant disciple (1 Cor. 9:27). Attempting to reform the flesh is a losing and futile battle to be won by the flesh without exception. But, But, But ..... **"But thanks be to God, which giveth us the victory through our Lord Jesus Christ."** (1 Cor. 15:57)

> **"For if by one man's offence death reigned by one; much more they which receive abundance of grace and of the gift of righteousness shall reign in life by one, Jesus Christ.)" Romans 5:17**

The abundant grace or divine enablement is ever present in us through Christ, our Great Intercessor, to conquer all sin and ride above it on the wings of His perfect priesthood and communion with us (Heb. 3:1; 4:14-16; 7:24-26; 1 Jn. 1:3; 5:4-5). Such victory is accomplished **"through the Spirit"** of God that dwells in us, His temples in which He dwells (Rom. 8:13; 1 Cor. 3:16). As we partake with Him, ever hungering and thirsting for His righteousness, He fills us – His very vessels – and all iniquity is put far from our tabernacles as He glorifies Himself in us in communion and fruitfulness (Job 22:21-13; Matt. 5:6; 2 Cor. 4:7). God be praised forevermore through Jesus Christ our LORD!

Here are the tools He granted His Church, that we might realize that victory (Acts 1:8; 2:4; Rom. 8:26-27; Jude 20).

> "The Holy Spirit is purposely given to intercede for me in prayer." Andrew Murray

PRAYER: *Father, please propel me by Thy grace and Spirit to the cross – to suffer the death of the self-life, that Christ Himself might reign supreme in this life You have given. Anoint me to the burial of the old man that You alone might be fruitful and victorious in this vessel of Your honor. Bless all Your saints the world over, to know You in the power of Your resurrection and fellowship of Your sufferings. In Jesus' holy name. Amen.*

Capture Points

- Discuss 1 Corinthians 15:51-58 and the ultimate victory of Christ over sin. How will this affect all believers?

- On an index card, write out 2 Timothy 2:11-12 (KJV recommended).

- What is the mind of Christ revealed in Romans 8:13?

- Discuss the important subject of deceivers, false prophets, and false teachings from 2 Cor. 11:2-5; 12-15; Gal. 1:6-10; Jude 3-4, etc.

SafeGuardYourSoul.com

Addendum

Making Peace with God

"But your iniquities (sins) have separated between you and your God, and your sins have hid his face from you, that he will not hear." Isaiah 59:2

God is holy and our sins separate us from Him. We have all broken God's laws by lying, dishonoring our parents, cheating, hating, committing a sex act in our mind with someone we are not married to, stealing, coveting, taking His holy name in vain, etc. These are all sins against God and we are all guilty. *Committing any single one of these sins makes us guilty of breaking the whole law and worthy of death.*

Divine justice demands that our violations be punished. Because we are guilty of breaking God's holy law, we deserve to be fairly repaid for our offenses. God doesn't want us to be punished in hell forever though, so He sent His Son to pay the debt for us, so we would not have to pay for our own sins in eternal hell as we clearly deserve, but rather live now and forever with Him. What love!

At the end of a perfect (sinless) life, Christ carried the very cross He was to be nailed to. His infinite love for you, along with the nails driven through His hands and feet, held Him to that cross as He agonized for 6 hours in pain - to pay for your sins. He was crucified to make peace between God and man. The Son of God bridged the gap that sin had caused. This wonderful man named Jesus chose to shed His life blood (die - in excruciating pain) for you rather than live without you. He loves you.

> **"For the wages of sin is death; but the gift of God is eternal life through Jesus Christ our Lord." Romans 6:23**

Christ died to fully pay for the sins of the human race (John 19:30). God loves all men and wants us to experience relationship with Him, now and forever (John 17:3). Friend, who else has ever died for you but Jesus, the Good Shepherd?

> **"For when we were yet without strength, in due time Christ died for the ungodly (that's you)." Romans 5:6**

> **"Christ Jesus came into the world to save (rescue) sinners." 1 Timothy 1:15**

No religion or religious figure can save your soul from hell (no matter what they claim). Jesus didn't come to start a religion but rather to establish His eternal kingdom in the hearts of men, granting them a relationship with God. Jesus Christ is the only One who bears nail-scarred hands and feet for your sins. He is the *only* way to God and your only hope.

"For there is ONE God, and ONE mediator between God and men, the man Christ Jesus." 1 Timothy 2:5

The Son of God died and rose again to take away all your sins. He was the only One qualified for the job and He is the only One worthy of your worship. Peace with God happens when we meet the Prince of Peace.

Now apply His holy blood to your life so that you may live now and eternally with Him. You must completely turn your life over to Him and turn away from all your sins - repent. Now, pray this prayer to God with all that is within you, from your heart and out loud: "Dear Lord Jesus, thank You for shedding Your holy blood for my sins to save me from eternal damnation in hell. You are my only hope. Heavenly Father, I acknowledge all my sins against You right now, and ask Your forgiveness through the precious blood of Jesus, who died and rose again for me. Lord Jesus, take over my life right now and forevermore. I love You. Amen."

Tell another Christian. Find a group of Christ-centered believers who love God's Word. Be water baptized. Read your King James Bible daily and talk with God in prayer. Follow Christ to the end of your life. Sign up for the free email devotionals at SafeGuardYourSoul.com.

ANOTHER TRACT FROM SAFEGUARDYOURSOUL

LOSER

Jesus told us all that only the losers will gain eternal life (Matt. 10:38-39). With the holy law to convict of sin, the necessity of "repentance toward God and faith toward our Lord Jesus Christ," and the holiness of our Maker emphasized, this Gospel tract has already blessed tens of thousands of souls with the knowledge of God. It's very well received among people. The ease of handing this one out is second to none. May God bless the conversations we are able to engage in when handing this one out to the lost and when supplying other Christians.

Find out more about this book at www.SafeGuardYourSoul.com

ANOTHER TRACT FROM SAFEGUARDYOURSOUL

Diary of a Dead Man

With the horrible cover image, this tract instantly grabs attention of the recipient. While handing it out, one may choose to ask, "That's a horrible image huh?" The person receiving the tract will then say, "Yes it sure is." To this the believer can respond with, "Please don't end up like that guy." This is also a very easy Gospel tract to distribute with wide and virtually flawless response and receptivity – sure to make your seed sowing journey very fruitful.

Find out more about this book at www.SafeGuardYourSoul.com

ANOTHER TRACT FROM SAFEGUARDYOURSOUL

JESUS: *Why Did This Man Die On A Cross?*

With millions in print, the JESUS Tract is reaching thousands of lost souls globally and is perhaps the most condensed and complete presentation of the holy law and Gospel available in tract form today. This tract contains a glorious exaltation of the **"Great Shepherd of the sheep,"** *the* **"Good Shepherd"** *who came to pay the complete price for the sins of His fallen creation (Heb. 13:20; Jn. 10:1-10). Order your supply today and begin using these messengers to reach those for whom He died and rose again.*

Find out more about this book at www.SafeGuardYourSoul.com

ANOTHER TRACT FROM SAFEGUARDYOURSOUL

SECRETS *From Beyond the Grave*

Shocking & thought-provoking secrets about the after life. Contains a blistering menu of what awaits all who are not born again. This message is not for those who wish to hide the whole truth about eternal things. SECRETS is a tract few can resist reading with its aesthetic wickedness which reeks of death, and curiosity provoking title.

Find out more about this book at www.SafeGuardYourSoul.com

Order Your Supply of Powerful Gospel Tracts Today at:

SafeGuardYourSoul.com

SafeGuardYourSoul

9201 Warren Parkway Suite 200

Frisco, TX 75035

469.334.7090

SHARPENING YOUR PERSONAL DISCERNMENT

For the Building Up of His Saints

To begin receiving the *Moments for My Master* email devotionals, sign up at SafeGuardYourSoul.com.

Also, sign up for print newsletter on site.

ANOTHER BOOK FROM SAFEGUARDYOURSOUL

LIE of the Ages
History's Fatal Falsehood

Lie of the Ages is a sound and extensive biblical expose' and annihilation of the first lie told to mankind – a falsehood that has rung through the corridors of history bringing devastation to all who believed it. This volume is a thorough revelation of why this dangerous, diabolical falsehood, still widely taught today, is so destructive to the eternal souls of men and the true Church of Jesus Christ.

740 Pages

Contains more than 57 life-changing chapters and prayers.

Find out more about this book at www.SafeGuardYourSoul.com

ANOTHER BOOK FROM SAFEGUARDYOURSOUL

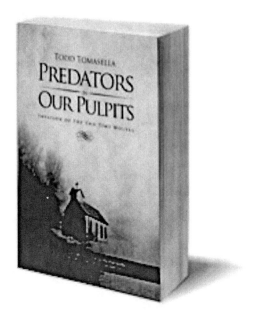

Predators in Our Pulpits
Invasion of the End Time Wolves

The prophesied great falling away is upon us – it's in our very "Christian" pulpits, books, and programs. As promised by our LORD and His apostles, "evil men and seducers" are waxing "worse and worse" in this late hour before our Savior's return (2 Tim. 3:13). Posing as ministers of righteousness, they have crept into the midst of biblically illiterate audiences on the wheels of their Trojan horse subterfuge and are promulgating poisonous pabulums in the pond of the heart of the people. These beguilers are depositing horrid heresies in the hearts of their hearers (1 Tim. 4:1-3).

Millions are becoming casualties of their war on the God of truth as they feverishly prey upon unlearned and unstable souls. Our only protection from the father of lies and his emissaries is to go deeper into the LORD ourselves, learning His truth and walking in the Holy Spirit. The contents of this volume will greatly enlighten the reader and direct his steps down the narrow road of light and truth, ever deepening His roots in the King of the soon coming, conquering and eternal kingdom of God .

What should the God-fearing do in response to this epidemic of evil that has invaded the modern church? How can we discern *who* and *what* teachings are true or false? Discover these answers in this timely, epic volume permeated with rarely revealed truth sure to nourish and sharpen any heart that hungers for more of Christ and His righteousness.

Find out more about this book at www.SafeGuardYourSoul.com

ANOTHER BOOK FROM SAFEGUARDYOURSOUL

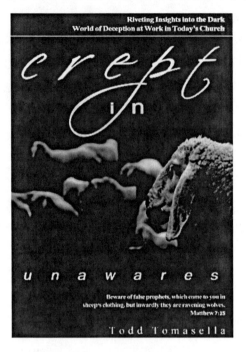

Crept in Unawares

> "For there are certain men crept in unawares, who were before of old ordained to this condemnation, ungodly men, turning the grace of our God into lasciviousness, and denying the only Lord God, and our Lord Jesus Christ." Jude 1:4

The subtlety of the enemy and **"the deceitfulness of sin"** is never to be underestimated by the enduring and abiding saint of Christ (Hebrews 3:12-14). This includes the

> **"And that because of false brethren unawares brought in, who came in privily to spy out our liberty which we have in Christ Jesus, that they might bring us into bondage." Galatians 2:4**

The enemy of our souls is active and aggressive in hunting down souls as he preys feverishly upon them, know his time is very short.

> **"Be sober, be vigilant; because your adversary the devil, as a roaring lion, walketh about, seeking whom he may devour." 1 Peter 5:8**

Find out more about this book at www.SafeGuardYourSoul.com

ANOTHER BOOK FROM SAFEGUARDYOURSOUL

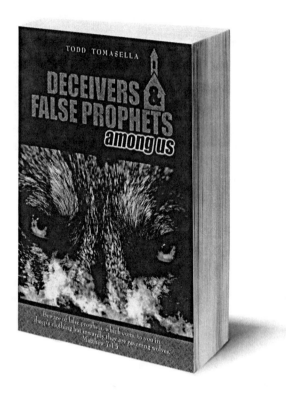

Deceivers *and*
False Prophets
Among Us

THE BOOK SOME LEADERS HOPE YOU NEVER FIND OUT ABOUT

Are there false, fruitless and even deceptive predators in the pulpits of the modern church? If so, are these deceivers leading multitudes to the worship of false gods through their damnable heresies? Are "seeker-friendly" churches creating a new class of "Christians" who have no concept of authentic, Biblical Christianity? Are there leaders who are building their own kingdoms in lieu of God's and doing so on your dime? Are we hearing the full-counsel of the LORD from those in leadership, or the psychology and programs of mere men? Are beguiling emissaries in our midst drawing believers away from pure devotion and intimacy with Jesus Christ? Do these things exist within your local fellowship? Are you truly being instructed in the right ways of the LORD? Explore the answers to these and many more questions in this bold, insightful, and resourceful look at the church world today.

WHAT YOU WILL GAIN FROM READING THIS BOOK:

o   What specific erroneous teachings are circulating in the church world and how to identify and expose them

o   How to discern the genuine leaders who truly follow the Word and Spirit of God, from the false and fruitless who are using God's money to build their own kingdoms

o   How to please the LORD by positioning and establishing His written revelation as final authority in your personal life

o   How to discern and cease wasting your brief existence on this earth supporting wolves in sheep's clothing

o   How to serve God with a loving and concerned heart from the foundation of divine immutable truth

278 Pages

Find out More about this book at www.SafeGuardYourSoul.com

For the latest resources, please visit
www.SafeGuardYourSoul.com

ANOTHER BOOK FROM SAFEGUARDYOURSOUL

Soul Damning Sins

Are there sins listed in God's Word that will damn ones soul to eternal hell? This is shocking revelation sure to strike the fear of God in the hearts of any who dare read this brief book. Great to read and to order copies to give away to others.

Find out more about this book at www.SafeGuardYourSoul.com

ANOTHER BOOK FROM SAFEGUARDYOURSOUL

"I Die Daily"
1 Corinthians 15:31

Here is some of what you will learn in the pages of this volume:

- *How to sink down deep into the death and burial of Christ, that God might raise you upward to bear abundant fruit for His glory*
- *The importance of loving and honoring the LORD above self, and seeing His grace and power work in you in ministry to others*
- *How to discern which leaders are teaching the truth from the many wolves among us*
- *How to incorporate the cross in your personal life daily, and live a life fully pleasing to God*

Find out more about this book at www.SafeGuardYourSoul.com

ABOUT THE AUTHOR

May the LORD do His ever-deepening work in each of us, perfecting that which concerns us, as He, our Potter, molds us – His clay – into His holy image (Jeremiah 18:1-6; Romans 8:29).

Todd Tomasella is a publisher of Gospel literature designed to strike the lost with the fear of God and to build up the body of Christ. Based in Dallas, Texas, Todd is blessed to possess divine grace with a kingdom perspective as he serves through discipleship-pastoring and evangelism on a daily basis and in local fellowship, Scripture-intensive books, Gospel tracts, the website SafeGuardYourSoul.com, the *Moments for My Master* email devotionals, and speaking engagements

Without Christ, Todd can do **"nothing."** (John 15:5)

Visit www.SafeGuardYourSoul.com

SHARPENING YOUR
PERSONAL DISCERNMENT

For the Building Up of His Saints

To begin receiving the *Moments for My Master* email, sign up at SafeGuardYourSoul.com. OR, send your request to: info@safeguardyoursoul.com

Order Your Supply of Powerful Gospel Tracts Today at:

SafeGuardYourSoul.com

SafeGuardYourSoul

9201 Warren Parkway Suite 200

Frisco, TX 75035

469.334.7090

CPSIA information can be obtained at www.ICGtesting.com
Printed in the USA
LVOW081610030113

314242LV00009B/1010/P